BUSINESS RESCUE

How to Fix a Company that is Losing Money

AL ROSEN

BUSINESS UNIVERSITY PRESS
1170 Blue Gum • Anaheim • California 92806

Manufactured in the United States of America.

Library of Congress Cataloging in Publication Data

Rosen, Al

Business Rescue

How to Fix a Company that is Losing Money.

1. Business-Management. 1. Title

1988 936.9 88-071555

ISBN: 0-9620675-0-4

DEDICATION

This book is dedicated to all those managers and entrepreneurs who have gone through a turnaround. Only they can fully understand the pain of failure and the joy of success.

ABOUT THE AUTHOR

Al Rosen was born in Philadelphia in 1938. He relocated to the Los Angeles area in 1961, where he now resides. He spent most of his early years in various selling assignments, working his way up through the management ranks until he eventually became the president of a check printing company with more than 200 employees.

Al Rosen is currently the president of a specialized consulting firm that helps businesses with problems in sales, production, organization, and finance (operating at a loss). His client list is international in scope and includes a wide range of industries. A popular member of the West Coast lecture circuit, he gives seminars and speeches on "Business Rescue," as well as finding, hiring and managing salespeople.

Al Rosen can be reached at his firm:

The Business Rescue Group
2535 Skyline Drive
Brea, California 92621
(714) 990-3039

ACKNOWLEDGMENT

My very special thanks to my wife, Gaynell, whose encouragement and support were essential to the writing of this book. Thanks also to all the other people who helped me with this project, especially Carole Morgan, who greatly helped with design and editing. Carole owns and operates The Morgan Association advertising/public relations firm, P.O. Box 839, La Quinta, CA 92253, 619/564-4807.

BUSINESS RESCUE

HOW TO FIX A COMPANY THAT IS LOSING MONEY

CONTENTS

BUSINESS RESCUE
How to Fix a Company that is Losing Money

FOREWORD

Over one million companies will close their doors in the "1990's." Most of them will be small businesses. How you, the entrepreneur, manage the up and down business cycles during your company's life span will determine the difference between success and failure.

In the last few years I have witnessed a strange phenomenon. There are more companies filing for bankruptcy than ever before, yet no one seems to be alarmed. Perhaps this can be attributed to the proliferation of new enterprises entering the marketplace.

For example, in the 1950's new businesses started at the rate of about 60,000 to 70,000 per year. Today the rate of new start-ups has increased to 600,000 or 700,000 per year — a 1,000% growth.

With so many new competitors in the marketplace, it has become increasingly difficult to generate a profit within a small business environment. Let us examine some specifics.

Because of the growth in start-up operations, there is much more competition. It used to be that a typical small company had some degree of exclusivity, or at least there was not the same kind of business on every corner as there is today. When a particular small business was the only one of its kind in the area, it was allowed to price the product or service with relation to the financial needs of the operation without too much concern for efficiency or productivity. In this environment, the management could get away with a great many errors in running the affairs of the firm and still end up with a profit. The fact is that it was significantly easier to make a profit years ago.

Other elements present today are the ever-changing labor market and the changing attitudes of the work force. How many times have you heard it said that employees are different today? Have you noticed that they simply do not seem to care as much as they did in the past? It appears that all they want is more money, less responsibility and more leisure time.

The most critical element of the economy has also changed. That element is the banking/financing part of managing a firm. It used to be that a small business could easily finance its efforts. This is not the case anymore. It used to be much easier to get a loan. Again, this is not true today. In fact, it has become almost mandatory for an owner to personally sign for even the smallest short-term loan.

What are the effects of inflation? During a period of double digit inflation, the pricing philosophy itself becomes a mask hiding the real problems of poor management. It was easy to raise prices, pay higher wages, borrow money, and revalue the inventory. These devices were good moves for those times. Unfortunately, the adverse effects of inflation are hidden because the real problems of the firm go unattended. When inflation comes under control, management problems will surface. Often they show up as an operating loss. In a stable economy, prices are not easily raised and losses cannot be regained through price increases. Therefore, other measures are needed to bring back the profits. Cash flow difficulties frequently appear simultaneously with operating losses. As a result, the company usually has trouble paying its bills.

Normally, other important elements must also be taken into consideration. Due to operating losses, suppliers, creditors, and employees must be dealt with. The aftermath of sustained financial losses will also affect the company's banking relationship.

When this combination of events occurs, management usually realizes that something is wrong, particularly when it becomes difficult to repay loans or make payroll. They must consider a turnaround philosophy if the business or its assets are going to be saved.

The word "turnaround" itself does not express the severity of a company's condition. It merely notes that something should be fixed or operating losses must be reversed.

Business Rescue *addresses most aspects of a turnaround. The text will cover the basic philosophy and seven major elements involved in a successful repair. It is designed for the reader to focus on all or any part of the steps, depending upon your needs or the particular problems. If properly applied, you may not become a casualty of the "1990's."*

Al Rosen
Brea, California

PART ONE

PRELIMINARY REVIEW

Chapter 1

ANALYZING THE REAL PROBLEMS OF THE BUSINESS

Before planning a strategy for a turnaround, ask yourself three important questions:

1. Is the business sick or is it only going through some temporary bad times?
2. Can the present management repair the problems or must there be a change?
3. Would it be better to sell the business?

Now, to examine these questions in detail:

DISCOVERY PROCESS

Is the business really sick? This question cannot be answered easily. There are many factors contributing to what may appear as the symptoms of a sick organization. It may be truly sick. Then again, to what degree? Is it terminally ill? In other words, is bankruptcy or liquidation inevitable?

Looking at historical information is one method often used to determine what is truly going on. For example: How long has the perceived distress existed? Certainly if the troubles started just a few months ago, then maybe it is only a temporary "bad times" condition. Nonetheless, even if this is the case, the symptoms should not be ignored. Remedial steps should be taken because it is not possible to tell how long the bad times will last. Often, sick businesses get distressed because their company or industry goes into an extended period of severe "bad times."

As a rule of thumb, even temporary troubles should be examined. That is not to say that every time a financial statement shows a little down trend or loss the management should go into a shock treatment mode to fix the condition. Still, any down trend or losses should be understood and explained. If the same condition continues, then something should be done. It will not go away by itself. There is, however, a definite management style that supports the theory that says, "Leave things alone long enough and they'll fix themselves." Not always true! Most of the time the dilemma gets worse. Strange as it sounds, problems often appear to have gone away. But, in reality, they do not go away.

Here is what happens to them: The symptoms do go away, or, more accurately stated, they change. The underlying difficulty is still there. Sometimes it is buried so well it appears to all concerned that the trouble has fixed itself. This is common with personnel problems (which are covered later in this book).

How can you tell how ill the company actually is? Is it sick enough to require a serious turnaround mode? There are signals or signposts that can point to where you can find the answer. One signal is poor cash flow. Do not confuse this with the knowledge that all small enterprises suffer to some degree from the lack of cash flow. The sign to look for is a change in cash flow — for the worse.

Suppose your enterprise has always had money problems. Then, all of a sudden or over a short period of time, the problems accelerate. The bills get more and more difficult to pay. Perhaps some suppliers are threatening to put the organization on a cash on delivery (C.O.D.) basis. The business starts having trouble repaying its bank obligations. Other cash flow problems surface that seem to be worse than ever before. By the way, some firms ignore this important signal and borrow more money to ease the pressure. It is a sure indication that a turnaround is necessary when the lending sources refuse to advance more funds. Still, some entrepreneurs refuse to believe it. They will even lend the business the money themselves, if they have any to lend.

There are other equally important signals. One, for example, is declining sales. Sales are the life's blood of any business. Sales are the source of incoming revenue. Logically, if sales drop, eventually so does revenue. Measuring or discovering a possible down trend in sales is easy if you have records. The decline in sales may be so obvious that no comparisons are necessary. Then again, the sales loss could be seasonal or only temporary. Looking at historical sales trends can be helpful because it can take the confusion out of what the information says.

Looking at sales figures in an organized way can teach you much. The following example is one way you can look at a sales picture:

CURRENT MO.	LAST YR.	%	Y.T.D.	LAST YR.	%
$42,688.	**$44,819.**	**-4.75**	**621,300.**	**637.450.**	**-2.5**

The example clearly shows a trend. The year-to-date sales are down 2-1/2%. The current month is down even more than the year-to-date figure by almost double the percentage. All indications here point to an accelerating downward sales trend. Look at all months in the same manner. If, for the most part, the entire report looks the same way (month by month), then obviously sales are actually declining.

Sometimes the monthly sales trend can be misleading. It may not consider seasonal factors, which is why comparing this month's sales with last month's sales is not a wise method for forecasting trends. The proper comparisons should always be for the same period this year with the same period last year.

If the business continues to show declining sales, then it won't be long before the reduced revenue takes its toll. This, of course, makes the assumption that expenses do not get adjusted in a timely fashion when there is a declining sales trend. The most common reason is that the expense relationship to declining sales is ignored, and expenses may even increase.

There are a few other signals that can point to trouble. Inventory shortage is a good clue to possible problems. An inventory shortage occurs when a physical inventory is taken and there is less inventory on hand than what the books have recorded.

A monthly inventory figure is compulsory for calculating the cost of goods sold. But many organizations do not count inventory monthly. When there is no monthly ending and beginning inventory figure, an estimated gross profit calculation is used. This calculation is an assumption.

If the past period's gross profit was a certain percentage, then the same gross profit percentage is assumed for the current period. When physical inventories are not taken monthly, the shortage will surface. The discrepancy usually occurs when the inventory is counted on a quarterly, semi-annual or annual basis. That value was calculated based on several months of assumed gross profit. If that profit was really less than stated, an inventory shortage will result.

When an inventory shortage becomes known, the first thought is that someone has taken some of the inventory. This is natural for management to assume. But realistically, most of the time theft is not the culprit. Except for the occasional embezzlement, the real cause is the gross profit calculation. It is inaccurate monthly statements taken for fact, even though they may be wrong. The natural tendency is to think someone took inventory rather than believe that the financial statements are in error. Besides, it is not management's fault if someone steals the inventory. Moreover, management does not have to take responsibility for the real problems of the organization once there is a likely excuse.

The inventory was not taken illegally. The shortage is due to declining gross profits, another indication of serious problems.

UNDERSTANDING GROSS PROFIT

Simply stated, gross profit is the difference between what it costs to produce or purchase a product and what the product sells for. As an example, suppose you pay $1.00 for your product and you sell it for $2.00. The gross profit is $1.00. The gross margin is 50%. You arrive at the percentage by dividing the cost by the selling price, then subtracting the remainder from 100. (Gross Margin equals 100 - [COST / SELLING PRICE]).

Since gross profits are the real income of the business, they should be as high as possible. The higher the margins, the greater the potential for profit. This is the reason that declining gross margins are a definite symptom of difficulties. Just like sales, these margins should be monitored and trended. Let us look at our sample comparison worksheet with gross margins added:

CURRENT MO.		LAST YR	%	Y.T.D.		LAST YR.	%
$42,688.		$44,819.	-4.75	$621,300.		$637,450.	-2.5
35,858.		35,407.		509,466.		497,211.	
$ 6,830.	16%	$ 9,412.	21%	$111,834.	18%	$140,239.	22%

The first line represents the sales. The second line is the cost of the materials or products (cost of goods sold). The second line is subtracted from the first and the remainder becomes the gross profit – the third line.

The worksheet decidedly shows declining gross profit margins. The current month shows the margin at 16% compared with 21% for the same month last year, a drop of 5% in the same month. The year-to-date margins have also declined by 3%. Compared with the current month's 5%, this suggests an accelerating decrease in margins. Lastly, last year's year-to-date margin was 22% compared with this year's 18%. Once again, there is a clear indication that gross profit margins are declining.

The example also shows a moderate decrease in operating profits. The net effect of this decrease is possible net losses. Sustained net losses can lead to cash shortages, which, for the most part, a small business cannot easily handle.

To review, the signals or symptoms which indicate that a turnaround strategy is necessary are:

1. Increasing cash flow problems
2. Decreasing sales trends
3. Inventory shortages
4. Decreasing gross profit margins
5. Large financial statement losses

The question of turnaround necessity is not the issue. Obviously, some of the most seriously distressed businesses may not be viable candidates for a turnaround. They may be a bankruptcy waiting to happen. On the other hand, the least severely stricken businesses may be saved easily. Setting aside these extreme polarities, there is still the vast in between.

The strategies discussed in this book are meant for those companies considered, by our definition, in between. These ideas are sound managing principles. They are, however, slanted. This is not a general guide book for good management techniques. Many of the possible solutions presented here are remedial, not preventive. However, any organization could make good use of this information. Ideas that could improve performance should always be welcome.

CONSIDER A CHANGE

The second question was: Can the present management turn the business around, or do they need to bring in someone else to do the job? These are the advantages and disadvantages of each decision.

First, the advantage of bringing in someone new is that they have a fresh approach to the task. They will look at all aspects of the problem and understand the necessary urgency. They know it will not get better by itself. They also will not be handicapped or daunted by previous failures. They will try options that the existing management thinks will not work. Amazingly enough, they do. For example:

A printing company did not bill their customers freight or delivery charges. All shipments were F.O.B. destination, including the out-of-state delivery. The existing management felt that charging for delivery would hurt sales. "Besides," they said, "our competition does not charge freight either."

The company hired a new Chief Operating Officer (COO) who started to make the changes necessary for a turnaround. One area he focused on was the freight issue. From his past experience he knew that most companies charged the customer freight. He told his subordinates that additional profits could be made if the company charged the customer for delivery. The sales force affected had a fit. They argued that this would lose orders and upset customers.

The COO listened, then decided that more research was necessary before making a decision. He asked one of his secretaries to call all the competition in town pretending she was a potential customer. She asked about free delivery, credit terms, delivery times, and a host of other questions that would give him some idea of what was going on in the marketplace.

The information she received was revealing. The COO learned that 80 percent of the competition charged the customer for delivery. He showed the results of the survey to his management team, and they still refused to believe it. However, because of his own determination, he was able to win over some managers. They were willing to try charging for delivery, but with one condition: If any customer complained about the charges, the company would, without any quarrel, issue a credit memo for the delivery charges.

Within the following month only four credit memos were issued, and the month's delivery revenue was $12,000 net. In subsequent months the credit memos dropped to zero. Only on a rare occasion would a customer bring the subject up. Surprisingly, most of the customers did not realize that the company used to give free delivery.

In retrospect, the new manager was not smarter. He just wanted to fix the business and was willing to try something innovative. Once he became convinced, through his research, that it would do no harm to the company, he moved ahead. He did not let himself get talked out of it by his doubting subordinates. Resistance to new ideas is perfectly normal and expected. The manager who does not implement his ideas loses. This particular manager exercised his leadership and was successful.

New management brings other advantages also. A new face can often get some concessions from employees where the old management could not. And, as you will learn later, employee concessions are a necessary element.

There is always a brief "honeymoon" with new management. This "honeymoon," as short as it may be, can accomplish a great deal, especially when it comes to working with the suppliers in restructuring the debt. Also, new management can bring enthusiasm to the organization. This enthusiasm is very important.

One of the disadvantages of new management is the additional expense of having the new manager. Generally, this is not a low paid employee. Anyone qualified to do the job is going to require a compensation package worthy of his ability.

Another concern is the relationship between the new manager and the owner. The owner's ego can get in the way, even though the new manager is doing a good job. There can be a great deal of mixed emotions. It is like watching your worst enemy drive off a cliff in your new Cadillac. The good news is that the new manager is fixing the company. The bad news is that it can make the owner feel inadequate and like a personal failure.

Another disadvantage is not being able to find someone qualified to undertake a turnaround from within your own industry. Most likely the new manager will come from the outside. This means that he will not know your particular business. Therefore, it will take a certain amount of time and effort for him to familiarize himself with your company. It is not critical for the new manager to be knowledgeable about your industry, because most turnaround specialists know the basic elements well enough to function in any industry.

A good repair expert will find a knowledgeable subordinate to help with the technical end of running things. Remember, his value is not what he knows about your industry. His value is what he knows about fixing your organization.

Finding such a qualified person is difficult at best, so a compromise may be necessary. But be careful! The risk is great. It would be terrific if the person did have particular knowledge of your industry. But, given a choice between an experienced turnaround specialist or a knowledgeable person in your industry, choose the person with the turnaround experience.

There are numerous advantages and disadvantages of the owner or existing management trying to repair the operation. The owner has the most at stake. If he fails, then all is lost. So the motivation for being successful is extremely strong, if not overwhelming.

A second advantage is that existing management knows the most about the organization. Not only does the owner know his particular company, but he knows the industry conditions as well. This can also be a slight disadvantage, because the owner can be "too close to the forest to see the trees."

Another advantage is that the present management knows the people in the organization. They know their strengths and weaknesses and are less likely to put someone in a position unfit for their qualifications, although they may have already done that in some cases.

In addition, the owner or the existing managers have developed relationships with the customers and suppliers.

For every advantage, there are just as many disadvantages for the owner or existing management to try the turnaround. First, the cause of the present circumstance may be the owner's inability to successfully run the company, and, in the absence of outside help, he will not be able to fix the company.

What if the owner cannot motivate the people in his organization? Without a commitment from the employees, the repair will never happen. The employees may love and respect the owner and would probably do anything for him. This relationship can be very advantageous. On the other hand, what if the owner thinks the employees really love him when, in reality, they could care less?

The main disadvantage of the owner or existing management doing the necessary repairs is the amount of effort that is required, aside from the knowledge. Sometimes the owner is just burned out due to the overwhelming pressure. If management has lost the excitement or enthusiasm, how can they inspire the rest of the employees? They obviously cannot.

The alternative is to bring in an expert who could be second in command. Theoretically, this option sounds great, because the owner can still be in charge. Be cautious, though; if the second-in-command does not have hands-on experience, he can foul things up. Once a firm suffers major problems, there is no more margin for error. The wrong person applying the wrong techniques can be disastrous.

Another disadvantage of a "second-in-command " option is the division of authority. The owner will always, inadvertently, interfere. He is still the boss, and all the employees know it. This characteristic will surface when it becomes necessary for bold action, such as raising prices or cutting commissions. When there is no clear-cut line of authority, conflict will exist. All it takes is just a few incidents where the second in command is overruled. After that, it won't be long before the second in command gives up. He will either quit or, even worse, become nonfunctional.

As an alternative to bringing in a "second-in-command," the owner would be better advised to turn the operation over to a new COO. Another option is the use of a special consultant. Once again, there are advantages and disadvantages.

The major advantage is that you can hire the best without putting him on the payroll permanently. You only pay for what you get. The second advantage is that it still leaves the present management in control of the business.

A good consultant can be completely objective. He will not get emotionally involved. Therefore, his advice, if listened to, can be helpful. And since he is only making qualified recommendations, the final decision on any matter remains in the hands of the owner, providing the owner does not become emotionally paralyzed and unable to make important decisions.

The disadvantages include the added expense. A good consultant is expensive. It could turn out that you will pay more for a part-time consultant than a full-time employee. Also, the consultant is hired on a part-time basis. He has other clients and cannot devote all the time you might require. He may not always be there for you when you need him.

Finding an expert consultant is a task. Be sure that the person you hire has had substantial operational experience and not just teaching or consulting experience. There are times when you need a "numbers person;" someone who will do projections, cash flow forecasts, business plans, or pro formas. That is what many consultants do. But, when it comes to a serious turnaround, you need more than numbers and projections. You need day-to-day operational advice. More important, you will need a track to run on, a strategy. Once again, as this example shows, be careful of the traps.

A metal fabrication job shop got into financial trouble a few years ago. The president hired a well-known national consulting firm. He found them quite by accident. The consulting firm's salesman was out knocking on doors offering a free evaluation. The president gave the consulting firm a chance. Well, needless to say, their free evaluation was worth exactly what it cost, nothing. What came next was classic. They encouraged the president to purchase the next step, which was a written report — a type of a business plan (if you could call it that).

The president should have suspected that something was amiss because of their payment policy. They wanted to be paid in full before they even started the project. Two weeks later, they brought him a written report that told the president exactly what he had told the consultants. The report was a useless piece of junk. When the president complained, they said that he would have to purchase more of their services to get a report that made recommendations. He signed up again. And guess what? They wanted cash in advance as before. The next report was as useless as the first. Oddly enough, the consulting firm tried to get him to sign up for even more reports.

The metal shop spent thousands of dollars on consulting projects at a time when it could not afford to spend anything. All they ended up with was a series of written reports illustrating the company problems — information the officers and the Board of Directors already knew.

The horror story just described is a commonplace occurrence. Owners and managers with problems fall victim to these types of consultants. However, there are many good consultants out there that will not take advantage of you. You just have to weed out the bad ones to find a good one.

STRUCTURING A CONSULTING PROJECT

Most business situations are unique. As a consequence, each consulting project will be different. Nevertheless, there are some universal guidelines. For discussion purposes, a consulting project to repair an ill organization will be the only concern.

Negotiate a fixed amount of dollars for the project. Do not get involved with hourly fees. You can spend a great deal more than what you bargained for. Also, try to negotiate a small, flat monthly fee for a continuing relationship. If you feel the consultant has been helpful, suggest that he become a member of your Board of Directors. That is the least expensive way to acquire expert help.

Ask for the project in four phases. First, there should be a "scope analysis" to focus on the areas that seem to be out of line with either industry standards or profitable historic standards. This is a comprehensive diagnosis. Second, you will want a "target analysis" to determine what must specifically be done in each area defined as a target for major improvement. This is a detailed list of recommendations. Third, have an "implementation plan" drawn up to establish a detailed operations plan to remedy the defined target areas. This will include possible personnel and purchasing changes as well as procedure modifications. The plan will also spell out reasonable time frames for accomplishment. And last, set up a "monitoring system" to insure that repairs are made and recommendations are followed.

ANALYSIS OF PRESENT MANAGEMENT

So far the question has been whether the owner should try the repair by himself or bring in some help. Suppose the owner is not running the firm. Suppose someone else is in charge. Generally speaking, the present management may have to be dismissed. It is one thing for the owner to have messed things up. After all, it is his property. But to suffer from someone else's mistakes is not necessary.

If the present general manager is not the owner, why continue with him? Certainly not for sentimental reasons. Not when survival is at stake.

What about existing staff? Should they go also? Usually, the answer is "yes." But maybe that is too general a statement. Each condition must be judged on its own merit.

There are circumstances where the second-in-command should take over, especially if he was unable to do his job because his superior would not let him. By the way, this is common. Sometimes the second in command can really see the faults. Perhaps he has watched the downfall of the business but could not convince his superior to take defensive action.

There was a situation where the vice president of a distribution company was better suited to be the president. At the time the company was not having extreme difficulties. It was still making a profit, even though the profits were declining. The vice president knew what needed to be done. The president saw the necessity to take some positive action, but he did not have the vision to do the right thing (mainly because of a lack of that kind of experience). In the final analysis nothing much happened.

Out of frustration, the vice president wanted to leave the organization. Deep in his heart he felt a loyalty to the owner, and it was impossible to walk away. He felt that eventually the president would quit or get fired.

As it turned out, the vice president found another job with greater responsibility and was a substantial success in his new career.

This was clearly a case where the second in command should have been elevated, but it did not happen. The company was just not in bad enough shape to force that development.

Four years after the second-in-command left, sales had gone down almost 25% and the profits slid down to nothing. This forced the owner to put the company up for sale. Four years earlier the owner should have fired the president and put the vice president in charge. Maybe the result would have been different.

You may have to get rid of a bunch of managers. But first, get yourself a new Chief. Let him do the honors, and, of course, let him find the replacements as well. In some cases, the new manager may even have his own team ready to move in.

The final decision rests with the owner. Because there are so many factors involved, much thought should be given to all the conditions before a good decision can be made. Before moving on, here is a review of the options available to the owner:

- Bring in someone else to do the repairs.
- Look at the existing management team for a new leader.
- Fix the business himself, if he can.
- Bring in a consultant to guide the turnaround.

The difficult part is the realization that the owner is not omnipotent and that seeking other options may be better. To reiterate, no matter what option is ultimately chosen, a commitment must be made to tackle the problems with great energy and enthusiasm. A turnaround requires an excited leader who can get his management team excited as well. When this happens, a synergy occurs, and what may seem to be the impossible becomes attainable.

CONSIDER SELLING OUT

The third question was, "Would it be better to sell the business?" This is the most difficult question of all since the answer will come from the owner's subjective feelings. The emotional ties to his business transcend rational objectivity.

In some situations the owner feels that the business is his child. He will often say, "This company means more to me than it would to someone else. I've got an awful lot in this. How is anyone else ever going to understand the sweat and blood I put into this?" He will also say, "I can't sell the organization in the condition it's in. I've got to fix it first."

In the extreme, some owners would rather sink than sell. This philosophy is, of course, not on a conscious level. Yet, the business should have been sold when there was still something to sell. In retrospect, selling out, at that time, was not thought to be a reasonable option. It is usually extreme pressure that ultimately starts the ball rolling toward selling the business.

There are times when the decision to sell comes too late. When that happens there is usually a mad scramble to prepare a business plan and find a buyer. This activity can even add to the dilemma, because the management efforts are focused toward selling the company instead of fixing the problems.

Selling a business takes time. It cannot be done overnight. The fast sale is an exception and often a disaster. It can take as long as a year to find a qualified buyer and make a sale. Waiting too long, meaning waiting until there are no other options, can be disastrous.

Selling out should always be a consideration even while you are implementing remedial steps.

What are some good reasons to sell? What should the motivation be? Aside from the losses and deteriorating conditions, what else could be a good reason to sell? Here are four basic considerations:

The first is insufficient capital. There may come a time when there is just not enough money available to support the continued losses, or growth for that matter. Even the borrowing has reached a limit. The profits are not what they used to be, and what is left is not enough.

Timing is the second reason. Maybe now is the best time. The selling price now could be the highest the owner will get. Continuing losses will only deteriorate the selling price.

In a similar situation, an owner was offered $2,000,000 in cash for his business (the depreciated net worth). The owner was insulted and refused.

The losses continued to pile up. He was told that every day he waited, the value of the business went down $10,000 (the losses were $300,000 per month). The owner was once again insulted. Finally, it became apparent even to this stubborn owner that a sale was the only way out. The result was bankruptcy, because there was not enough time to make a deal. The timing was close. Another month would have been enough time to close a sale.

In the end, the stubborn owner tried to sell out for about $700,000 paid over 10 years with no interest. Two years earlier he turned down $2,000,000 in cash. His pride got in the way and prevented him from realizing how critical the condition was. Given a choice now, the owner would jump at the first offer. Most of the time, 20/20 hindsight would lead us to do something different.

The third consideration for selling could be the personal guarantees that an owner has signed in order to borrow money or to get credit. Even though the enterprise may be a corporation, personal guarantees may have been required. It could be motivation enough just to get out from under those obligations. The reason is simple. Suppose the company does not make it. The owner may lose his entire personal life savings.

The last reason is the human resource factor. Even though egos may get involved, there is still one question you must answer. Can the owner do it? Will the effort pay off, or is it better to get what you can now and let someone else worry about the problems?

An interesting phenomenon happens when a new owner gets involved. The new owner comes in with an enthusiasm and courage that has been lost or beaten out of the old owner. The new owner brings to the party new ideas and new people. The new owner will do things that the old owner assumes will not work. Yet somehow they do work, and work well.

The essence of the matter is simple. The present owner and his management team may not be emotionally capable to continue with the turnaround. The hardships that have brought the operation to its present state may have taken their toll on the people in the organization, especially the owner. Realistically, the owner should consider selling as an option, as opposed to trying to fix it himself and failing.

REVIEW

To summarize, the four considerations discussed for selling the business are:

1. The business needs capital that the owner cannot fund.
2. More money can be gotten now than later.
3. The personal guarantees could be removed.
4. There are not enough human resources to do a turnaround.

Subjectively, there may be a hundred other valid reasons for selling. Only the owner can know why he wants to consider this option. The main issue is the process used in making the decision. The decision should be made without a person's ego getting in the way. A decision must be just as good as it would be with 20/20 hindsight. When all is said and done, if you choose to sell, you will need to know the most expeditious and efficient way to do it. The next chapter illustrates one of the methods that works.

Chapter 2

HOW TO SELL THE BUSINESS IF NECESSARY

After looking at all of the pros and cons in Chapter 1, you may decide to sell the business rather than try a turnaround. You should be warned that a depressed company will sell for less than a prosperous one. Knowing your own feelings best, you may still decide to sell. If this is the case, then you will need to know how to go about doing it.

Your first thought may be to contact a business broker. Perhaps someone you know once told you they would be interested if you ever wanted to sell. Maybe even your biggest competitor has shown interest in buying you out or merging with you. For the time being, put those options aside and look at some hard facts. For one, you are either experiencing some financial trouble, or your business is going down hill. Your financial statement may look bad as well. Anyone interested in buying your business will soon discover your dilemma, and they will behave as if it is a distress sale. A sale under those conditions will not usually yield a top price.

There is something you can do to enhance your position. Consider carefully the "presentation." If you tell a potential buyer that your firm is in "deep yogurt," the buyer may offer you next to nothing. He may even lose interest. The first rule of conduct is to present your opportunity as positively as possible. Do not hide the facts or lie, but do not kill your own deal in the initial conversations.

MARKETING THE PRODUCT

Your key to getting a qualified buyer as well as a fair price is how you market the sale of your firm. Think for a moment: how are other products sold? The first step is to identify the potential buyers. Who are they and how can you reach them?

You might think that the easiest way to sell the organization is through a business broker. Yes, a business broker is easy. But the truly good deals are never given to a broker. They are marketed by insiders or deal makers. Do not dismiss the use of business brokers. They can bring you a qualified buyer. Be cautious though. You may not want to give them an exclusive. That way, if you find a buyer on your own, you will not have to pay a broker's fee for nothing.

If you think about it, there are a great many prospects who would be interested in acquiring you operation. What about your competitors? Are there any competitors that would benefit by acquiring your organization? What about out-of-town competitors that would love to have a location in your area? Right now, without your knowledge, they could be thinking about opening a branch in your area. The start-up cost would probably be a great deal more than buying your operation.

Recently, at a lunch meeting, a small business owner mentioned to his insurance agent that he meant to sell his company. One thing led to another, and the insurance man told him that he knew of some physician clients that were looking for an investment in some enterprise. Even a tax loss would be attractive to them. The owner eventually sold the firm to these two physicians, and they retained the owner on a five-year contract at a great salary. A win/win situation for all. The point is this: You never know who can help you, so why not market the business the same way you would sell anything of value?

Newspaper ads are also an excellent way to find prospects. In major newspapers you will find a section in the classified segment called "Business Opportunities." Speaking of newspapers, how about the *Wall Street Journal*? That is usually a good place to pick up some prospects (the more the merrier).

BUILDING INTEREST

Let us assume you now have some people that have expressed interest by answering your ad. What now? Do you give them the pitch over the phone? Do you send them financial statements? They will ask for current and historical financial information, but do not give it to them just yet.

The best and most professional way to approach these prospects is to send them a proposal first. Later in this chapter you will see an example of a proposal. After that, you qualify them, meaning, you find out if they are in fact interested in buying your business or are just "Lookie Loos." You must also find out if they are financially qualified.

Once you are reasonably certain that you have a viable prospect, you must get them excited about your company. You can do that by giving them a very professional and enthusiastic tour of your facility. You might even have them make a few customer calls with you (without letting the customer know what is going on). Put on a "dog and pony show" for them. Sell them on the opportunity and the idea that your business is great. Absolutely do not appear depressed, and do not bad mouth your own company or industry. Do not tell them, "It's a dog-eat-dog industry and it's tough to make a buck."

When they ask you why you want to sell (and they will ask), make your reason positive. Be prepared ahead of time by thinking of a good reason that will make sense to a prospective buyer.

PRICING STRATEGIES

When it comes to price, there is no common formula that you can use. Realistically, what is the value of any investment? It is only worth what someone is willing to pay. There are, however, some guidelines on establishing the selling price. One method is tied to net worth. Another may be net worth and some good will. Good will is the subjective value that an owner places on his business because it is a going business. When there is no net worth, it could be all "good will." This all "good will" method for pricing is common when selling a medical practice or professional firm. Very often the selling price will be a percentage of the annual volume. There are some that are priced as a multiple of earnings. A few may even sell for a combination of net worth, a multiple of earnings, and some factor for "good will" or annual sales.

Another aspect in determining the selling price is terms. If it is a cash sale, the price is usually lower than a term sale. The more creative the terms, the higher the price. And finally, there are a host of tax considerations that make up the sale agreement. Some of these are simple, and others are much too complex to cover in this chapter. For example, if you take part of your payoff as a consulting fee, then that is a very desirable pre-tax expense for the new owner. Otherwise, he may have to pay you off with after-tax dollars. The more attractive the terms or tax advantages, the easier it is to sell the business.

These are important negotiation considerations between you and the buyer. Afterward, you can have your attorney or accountant go over the deal before you chisel it in stone. A word of caution: Some attorneys are deal breakers. It is just their nature to pick a deal to death. They believe that they are doing their job for their client. Be careful; they may lose sight of your goal in this matter.

A buyer and seller courted each other for months. They negotiated over a long period of time and both compromised on many issues. Finally, the buyer made a satisfactory offer. Then the attorneys for the buyer and seller met in a conference room. Within two hours, both attorneys reached an impasse on an issue that was not really critical.

Everyone left the conference room that day with a resolve not to make the deal. Two months later, both parties regretted what happened. Even the seller's attorney said that it could have been worked out. The net result was unfortunate. The owner ran out of money and was forced to liquidate.

Anyone interested in purchasing your holdings will want to feel comfortable about his return on investment. If you are losing money, it is going to be very difficult to show a new owner any kind of return. There are a few acceptable maneuvers you can use. One common ploy is the restructuring or recasting of your income statement. This is done by adding to the bottom line all the depreciation, owner's salary and owner's benefits. Add back any unusual one-time or non-related expenses. The net figure may be a profit, or at least a breakeven. Another way to create an illusion of profit is to show your income statement on a forecasted pro forma basis. Paint a rosy picture. Make your projections show a profit. After all, they are only projections.

MARKET THE PLAN

Enough said about price and attorneys. It is time to discuss the use of the proposal, or business plan as it is often called. When mailing it to prospects, you should include a very enthusiastic cover letter. As an example, on the following page is an actual cover letter used to attract out-of-state suitors:

SAMPLE LETTER

May 6

Mr. Olaf Wilson
National Supply Inc.
1234 Any Street
His City, And State 00000

Dear Mr. Wilson

Enclosed is a proposal I have prepared for your consideration. I feel it would be worth a few moments of your time to look it over.

My company could be a very promising and economical vehicle for you to enter the southern area marketplace.

National Supply Inc. is a first class company -- one I would like to be associated with. Because of this, my price and terms are very negotiable, and I would make it very easy for National Supply Inc. to acquire the ABC Company.

I am definitely going to either sell or merge with another company in the very near future. I would like to give Olaf Wilson the first right of refusal; therefore, a rapid response from you would be greatly appreciated.

Sincerely,

John Q. Smith
President

A mail merge program on a computer was used to personalize each letter. Thirteen of these letters were sent. Seven responded with sincere interest. The approach worked very well.

Before writing the proposal, you must build an outline in order to collect and organize your thoughts. The proposal should be simple yet realistic. Any figures mentioned or shown in the plan should be accurate to the best of your knowledge.

The outline supplied here is just that, a basic, simple outline. You can modify it to suit your own style and needs.

When you have finished the plan/proposal, you should have it carefully typed or typeset and placed it in a high-quality cover. The same principle applies to the framing of a picture; the dressing only compliments the art.

BASIC ACQUISITION PROPOSAL OUTLINE:

(Under the title acquisition proposal, type a few paragraphs describing the amount of money you need and, briefly, what the return will be and why.)

A. Description of the business

B. History of the company

C. The competitive environment

D. Financial history of the company

(Put a spread sheet here of sales and profits by year since you started; leave out the current fiscal year.)

E. Current income statement

(Show this year's income statement only in estimate form. Use real figures for the completed months and estimated figures for the rest of the fiscal year. You can be optimistic here. The next few months can be as good as you want.)

F. Exhibits

(Show projections here that illustrate the facts of your proposal.)

G. Specific changes in the income statement with investment

(Show new statement with significant changes and note why these things would occur with the additional investment; make sure you can justify whatever you say here.)

H. Pro forma statements for the next five years

(Put a spread sheet here with sales and profits by year for the following five years; be optimistic here.)

I. Summary

(Review facts and explain how a high return on the money invested can be achieved)

J. Assumptions

(State the assumptions that you have made about the exhibits and projections/predictions)

From this type of outline, you can now create a proposal/business plan or a sale/merger plan.

In order to help you further understand this principle, the following is an example of a completed, real-life proposal. The names, along with a few other things, have been changed for obvious reasons.

ACQUISITION PROPOSAL:

Acquisition Proposal

It is the desire of the owner to sell the entire company. The current owner would like to remain as an employee. The new owner will, most likely, be required to invest about $100,000. A small portion of the funds would go to the present owner as a down payment on the purchase. The majority would be lent to the business. The value of this infusion of capital could result in a return on investment of a minimum of 6.5% to a maximum of 120% annually on the infusion capital (see exhibits #1, 2, 3 and the summary).

Present Condition

The industry has gone through a difficult economic period during the past two years. In addition, ABC, Inc. acquired Jones Designs Company two years ago. This acquisition

(continued)

resulted in a severe financial set-back for ABC.

The industry is now on a strong recovery. It appears this comeback is due to the strong growth of the southern area residential and commercial building industry.

Recognizing this, the plan calls for a phase-out of Jones Designs. The result will be a substantial reduction in current operating expenses.

The timing is right for ABC to become a dominant force in the marketplace. However, the unfortunate circumstances described have depleted the company's resources, making it very difficult for the current owner to realize the potential.

Description of the Company

ABC Company, Inc. is a wholesale distributor of picture framing materials, supplies, tools, and equipment. They service companies and individuals doing picture-framing, including custom-frame shops, art galleries, commercial framing companies, artists, and photographers. The primary market is Texas, with auxiliary markets in Louisiana, Oklahoma, and Arkansas. There are, at present, eleven employees, including a general manager, administrative assistant, and a commissioned salesman.

ABC is incorporated with 100% of the stock owned by John Q. Smith and his family.

History

ABC was founded in October 1978 by John Q. Smith, with a capital investment of less than $10,000. At the time, the company had a very limited product line and two employees.

The immediate goal was to build a customer base by providing good, friendly, and knowledgeable service to the southern area picture framers.

In the beginning, the main sources of new sales were from mail outs, customer word-of-mouth and some personal sales

(continued)

contact by John Q. Smith. With rapid sales growth, the company expanded after one year from a 2,000-square-foot building to 5,000 square feet. Two years later, it moved to its current location. At first, it only occupied 8,000 square feet.

A year later, the operation needed an additional 2,000 square feet. At that time, the other half of the building became available, so it became necessary to lease the 6,000 square feet. A sublease tenant was found for the excess 4,000 feet. The sublease tenant was a customer, Mary Jones Inc. This company specialized in servicing the art and framing needs of corporate clients. Eighteen months later, Mary Jones, the owner, sold out to ABC. By this acquisition Jones Designs was formed.

The acquisition was a mistake, and the losses have been damaging. These losses are being dealt with now. The largest expense is the rent, which will end soon because the lease has almost matured.

During the six and a half years in business, ABC has developed a reputation as a full-line distributor of quality picture-framing products and services. Its main asset is the large and loyal customer base.

From the very beginning, the major weakness of the company has always been its under-capitalization. This has handicapped the buying power, especially in the area of import moldings, where a savings of 30% to 70% can be realized on purchases. With the debacle of the Mary Jones acquisition (later named Jones Designs Inc), the company resources were depleted even further. The net result is that the company cannot buy the most common items that are requested by the customer, thereby resulting in a loss of sales. As evidence of this, sales have decreased about 20% in the last six months.

Competitive Situation

There are two other distributors in the southern area similar

(continued)

to ABC. A brief description of each of these follows. These descriptions are only the opinion and observations of John Q. Smith.

1. South Wholesale Co. – This is a small family-owned-and-operated company with limited product lines. It has been in business for five years. Their weakness is their limited product lines in the area of wood molding, equipment, and supply items.

2. AAA Molding Co. – Two years ago they opened a Florida operation, and approximately one year ago opened a southern branch. They came on strong by hiring a sales force, providing free statewide delivery, and, of course, some price cutting. Their weakness is this marketing philosophy. It appears to be catching up with them. They recently eliminated much or all their sales force and free delivery.

Summary

During the past six and a half years, ABC Company has definitely established itself in the picture framing industry. In this time, they have developed a very good organization of employees, as well as a fine reputation with the customers and suppliers.

Over the next few years, the future of ABC can be very promising because of the economic growth in the southern area and the growing industry of picture framing. ABC Company will also make some positive internal changes, which will enhance the value of the investment.

In order to bring operational expenses in line with current sales, the following steps are being taken:

1. Reducing rent by eliminating the Jones Designs operation. This action will save $3,000 per month in rent and utilities, plus $1,500 per month in employees. Also, about $30,000 in inventory, fixtures, and equipment can be sold or converted into cash.

(continued)

2. A reduction in other payroll expenses by cutting back two and a half employees. This action will save the company about $1,500 per month.

3. Eliminating the out-of-state WATS lines will save $350 per month.

4. Cutbacks in entertainment, auto, and insurance expenses will save another $1,000 per month.

The impact of these expense-saving cutbacks will net about $7,350 per month to the bottom line. These actions will render a small profit on a pro forma basis – somewhere between $12,000 and $20,000 annually.

These actions will also bring the monthly operating expenses to break-even at a monthly sales level of $53,000. The current average is $58,000. Even at the worst sales scenario, the company will be operating at break-even within sixty days.

Looking at it positively, sales should increase to an annual level of $828,000, as illustrated in exhibit #2. The intent is to keep expenses at a minimum thereby maximizing the return on investment. The expenses are calculated on a corresponding percentage basis. Naturally a more conservative operating attitude could produce an even higher return than the projections illustrate.

It was stated that the investment required would be about $100,000. Most of the investment will become an asset of the business and not used to purchase the company. The following items are places where the investment can yield the quickest return:

- Acquisition of one of the competitors in the area
- Reduction of bank debt at 14% interest
- Special purchases at higher gross margins
- Increased marketing and sales programs
- Acquisition of certain inventory necessary to bring sales back to previous levels

(Continued)

The five-year projection shown in Exhibit #2 does not include a specific investment. However, the five-year projection in Exhibit #3 illustrates the impact of the investment by allocating it to reducing the bank debt and making some special purchases.

The bottom line on Exhibit #3 shows the impact of the investment. The projection without the infusion of capital shows a net profit in the fifth year of $88,346, whereas the projection with the capital infusion shows a net profit of $117,828 in the fifth year. The result is a 33 % net effect.

The real impact of the investment is illustrated in the cumulative profit projections. With the investment of $100,000, the cumulative net profit is more than 50% greater than the projection without the $100,000 investment. It also shows a total of $134,024 more net profit. This amount should compare to the original investment of $100,000. That equates to an additional 134% return over five years.

Assuming the money is used for an acquisition, the comparison should be between Exhibit #1 and Exhibit #2. The five-year cumulative net profit with an acquisition is $869,216 compared with the cumulative net profit without the investment of $267,427. The net difference is $601,789 additional profit – a gain of about 600% on the original investment of $100,000.

Assumptions

(Each of the following exhibits should be supported by a representative spreadsheet.)

Exhibit #1:

1. Sales are forecasted at a 10% annual increase compounded.

2. Expenses are budgeted at the same percentage as current operations with a 5% annual increase compounded.

3. The first year sales is a combination of the sales of ABC

(continued)

Company and either of the two competitors' guesstimated sales.

4. Gross margins are stated at 40% (the company's present level).

<u>Exhibit #2</u>

1. Sales are forecast at an increase of 15% the first year and 10% each year thereafter (compounded).

2. Gross margins have been increased to 43%.

3. Expenses are budgeted at the same percentage as current operations with a 5% annual increase compounded.

<u>Exhibit #3</u>

1. Sales are forecast at a 15% increase the first year and 10% each year thereafter (compounded).

2. Expenses are budgeted at the same percentage as current operations with a 5% annual increase compounded.

3. Gross margins have been increased to 45%.

4. The bank debt is reduced by 50% from its present value in the first year.

Summary

The facts, figures, and predictions stated in this proposal are the opinions of the owner of ABC Company, John Q. Smith. It is his sincere belief that what is represented here is true, to the best of his knowledge and experience. However, this proposal rests on opinions and predictions, and, although prepared with the best intentions, these predictions may not come to fruition.

COMPETITIVE INFORMATION

After you have given the proposal to several prospects, you will start to get some serious interest. A word of caution: Be careful that you do not give valuable, competitive information to anyone who could use this information against you.

A shrewd entrepreneur was negotiating for the acquisition of his major competitor. In essence, he was only interested in learning about his competitor's accounts and other operating secrets. The result was that he did not acquire the organization. He did, however, hire quite a few of his competitor's salesmen and a couple of his managers.

In another situation, while the potential buyer was performing his due diligence, he was gathering competitive information such as accounts receivable aging lists and accounts payable lists. The sale didn't mature, but the competitor acquired a great deal of information which he eventually used against the seller.

Bearing this in mind, when do you give important information to a prospective buyer? It is a matter of timing. You certainly do not want to give everything you have to mildly interested parties. Use the proposal to build interest, not to reveal your operating secrets. Then, when you are convinced that you have a serious buyer, give him a balance sheet and current income statement. Anything beyond that is performance of due diligence. That is not done on speculation. A letter of intent or written offer usually precedes the performance of due diligence. Price and terms must be agreed upon conceptually before due diligence is performed by the potential buyer. The less he looks, the fewer the chances for something to go wrong.

REVIEW

To summarize the steps involved in selling the business:

1. Identify your potential buyers or prospects.
2. Prepare a proposal or presentation.
3. Sell or market the potential of the business.
4. Be positive and have a good reason for selling.
5. Control the process of the sale.
6. Do not give competitors valuable or damaging information.
7. Do not let attorneys ruin the deal.
8. Do not let the buyer see more than is necessary.
9. Keep the whole process simple.

Many sales fall apart at the eleventh hour. Do not get hung up on small details, and do not fall over dollars to pick up pennies.

PART TWO

GETTING STARTED

Chapter 3

THE IMPORTANCE OF HAVING ENOUGH TIME

A business repair program or the sale of the company is virtually impossible to achieve if there is not enough time. No matter what management can successfully accomplish, it takes time for the results to make an impact on operations. Sometimes a sale or turnaround can happen fast. Even so, you still need a minimum amount of time to make it stick.

If you sell out, it will take a minimum of 30 and up to 90 days before a sale can be completed. Even in a lightning-fast turnaround, at least 30 to 60 days are necessary before things get back to break even or profitability. Besides, it takes still more time to repair the damage. For example: Suppose the company is on COD. It may take six months to a year before the suppliers give open credit again. As a consequence, you must recognize time as an important commodity.

Almost all the ancillary people associated with your business, such as suppliers and bankers, are in opposition to your schedule. They do not want to give you any more time. They feel they have waited long enough. They want their money, and they are not prepared to consider any more stalling. They take that position because they do not see the big picture. If they did, they would approach your situation in a more cooperative mood.

You must convince these people that it takes time to plan, install, and operate a remedial program, and that the repair of the business is in their best interests also. They must give you the opportunity to put the company on a firm footing once again. This will be difficult to accomplish, but it is certainly not beyond a reasonable possibility. They may object, but they will give in, especially if they do not have much choice. Here is what will probably happen: They will give in, but they will insist on certain conditions. They may even request personal guarantees. That is also something you will have to deal with. In almost all cases they will want to see your plan. (This is covered in Chapter 16.)

There is a favorite story that illustrates the philosophy of time and the turnaround. A long time ago there was a King who became bored with his court advisor. The King summoned the advisor and said, "What have you done for me lately?" When the advisor could not tell the King anything new, the King told the advisor that he was going to put him to death.

Immediately the advisor said to the King, "Wait! Don't put me to death. I can do something really spectacular for you."

The King said, "What can you do that you haven't already done?"

The advisor then replied, "Your Highness, I can take your favorite, white horse and teach him to fly. And it will only take me one year to do it."

The King replied excitedly, "If you can make my horse fly, then I'll spare your life. But if you fail, I'll give you a terrible death — a death much worse than any you can imagine."

So the King spared the advisor's life. That afternoon the advisor's assistant asked the advisor why he had made such an insane bargain with the King. The assistant said, "You've only put off the inevitable. In a year the King will make you suffer even more. What have you gained?"

The advisor thought for a moment; then he said, "First of all, we've got a year that we didn't have before." He went on to say, "A lot of things can happen in a year. For one, the King could die. Two, I could die. And you know something else," the advisor said with a twinkle in his eye, "that horse might even fly."

MAKING DECISIONS

For the most part, turnarounds are easier than making a horse fly, but having enough time is crucial to making it happen.

Time is an important element for some of the obvious reasons stated. Time is, however, highlighted here for another reason. This book emphasizes many strategies that are focused toward either repairing the operation or buying more time. There are occasions when a poor, long-range decision must be made in order to buy some additional time now. Later, that short-sighted decision will hurt. But for now, it may keep the doors open another month. Some of the suggestions that are made in this book would not be good operating procedures if the business was really healthy. In fact, they would be considered poor judgment. In a turnaround, these decisions have to be made so that the business can have enough time to achieve the goals. Once that happens, many of these short-range strategies can be rethought.

TIME NEGOTIATIONS

There is a critical relationship between time and most repair strategies. You may have to buy time with certain employees or even a union. Without question, you'll need to get more time from the banks and most of the suppliers as well. This is a fairly simple process, but not easily accomplished. For example, with some suppliers you can even give them personal guarantees in order to buy some additional time considerations. Giving personal guarantees, at this point, may not have any meaning to you. You could be in so deep that if the business fails, so do you (personally).

Your major effort is developing an effective communication program with those that are interested and involved. A word of caution: First, be sure to have some defined plan of action that will make sense to the people you will be talking with.

The next step is to sell the feasibility of the plan. Show those interested what you are going to do and why their cooperation is absolutely necessary.

With leases you can renegotiate the terms. Give them some monetary advantage or pledge other equipment as additional security.

Unions and employees also have a strong motivation for you to succeed. It means jobs! Bare your soul to them and demand that they do their share. If they truly understand your predicament, they will cooperate; after all, what other choice do they have?

Irrespective of what you offer as an incentive, you must communicate with those parties on a friendly basis. Your goal is to buy time so that you can survive. If you do not survive, everyone loses, including your bankers, suppliers, and employees.

Throughout this book are many time-buying techniques and how you can apply them. Just keep in mind that buying time is absolutely critical.

A company that had severe financial problems preferred to sell out and not try a turnaround. The escrow took about 60 days. During that time, the company continued to have huge losses and, as a consequence, they ran out of cash. The bank foreclosed on their accounts receivable loan, even though there was an escrow in progress. The new buyer approached the bank to take over the loan, but the bank refused to do it without personal guarantees and additional collateral. The company could no longer make payroll or buy materials, so it was forced to close down. The new owner rescued the operation, but the price was renegotiated considerably downward.

There are two lessons to be learned from this story. The first one deals with the sale itself. Yes, there was a sale. Supposedly, selling solved all the owner's problems, at least, so he thought. Here is what went wrong: The owner did not try to run the organization in a turnaround mode. He did not think he had to any more; after all, the business was sold. Consequently, things got worse. Then it snowballed, and it was too late. The second lesson to be learned is that too little time is an enemy. Even though there was a sale, there just was not enough time to close it.

Using a 20/20 hindsight philosophy, the owner should have continued to run his business as if every day was critical. He should have realized that it would take time to complete the sale. Last, he should have communicated with his debtors. They could have surprised him, become supportive, and maybe even helped close the deal.

REVIEW

Here are the key issues:

1. Turnarounds cannot be made fast.
2. Decisions must be made that buy time.
3. Selling the business does not eliminate the need for time.
4. Time can be an enemy if it runs out on you.

Who knows? With a lot of hard work and some good luck, the horse might really fly!

Chapter 4

HOW TO RESTRUCTURE THE DEBT

Usually, when a business gets into financial trouble, the balance sheet looks terrible. The ratios are all out of kilter and upside down; and, because of that, most financial institutions will not lend the company more money. It appears that when things get bad, they seem to get worse by the hour. Bad news brings more bad news.

RATIOS

A word about ratios. Since financial institutions insist on using them as a yard-stick, you must understand what they are and how they are computed. Once you are comfortable with the technology, you can restructure the debt, and, thereby, change some of those measurement ratios.

The main ratio, if there is such a thing, is called the Current Ratio. This is calculated by dividing your current assets by your current liabilities. The meaning of current is more accurately stated as the most liquid of your assets and those liabilities that are short term, cash sensitive. Importance is given to this ratio because it can measure, to some extent, the liquidity of the company. It has been said by some accountants and bankers that a current ratio of 2.0 or better suggests that a company is probably healthy. This means that if you have twice as many liquid assets as current debt, you are in good shape. This is not entirely true, but some financial officials like to look at it that way. By itself, even financial gurus do not rely solely on the Current Ratio, or any ratio for that matter. They look at the total package. Poor ratios will affect, to some degree, how someone views your business financially, especially if you are losing money as well.

Debt-To-Net-Worth is another of the ratios. This is computed by dividing the total liabilities by the shareholder's equity. The higher the ratio, the worse shape the company is in. For example, suppose your liabilities are $600,000 and your equity, or net worth, is $300,000. The ratio is 2.0. Now, suppose that your net worth is only $150,000. The ratio is now 4.0.

Another ratio is the Total Debt-To-Current-Assets. This is computed by dividing the current assets by the total liabilities. Once again, the measurement is to see whether or not the operation has sufficient liquid assets to cover the entire debt. A ratio of 1.0 or higher will, supposedly, realize that objective. In running a business, it actually does not have much meaning unless you are planning to liquidate. Financial institutions like to look at that ratio because they may someday have to liquidate your company in order to get their loan repaid.

The Quick Ratio is a thumbnail measurement of the present cash flow. You compute this ratio by dividing the cash and accounts receivable by the current liabilities. A ratio of 1.0 says that you only have enough ready money to cover current debt. Any ratio less than 1.0 says that you cannot cover your obligations (hypothetically). By this reasoning, a ratio of 2.0 implies that you have twice as much as you need. This, of course, may not be true at all. Yet, this and the other ratios are given more regard than deserved. Because of that, you should pay some attention to them.

THE BALANCE SHEET

Owner frustration is not unusual. Anyone without the resolve to succeed will find it easy to just give up. That is the last thing you should do because there are several options still open.

The balance sheet is divided into two sections, assets and liabilities. Some liabilities are better than others. For example, long-term debt is better than accounts payable, because accounts payable is due now or, at best, 90 days from now. The cash will have to be available sooner, not later, whereas long-term debt does not drain the business of immediate cash.

On the assets side, "cash" is the best asset. Accounts receivable is better than inventory, because it can be converted to cash faster. Inventory has to be sold first. Most accounts receivable are collectible except for a small reserve for bad debt, whereas inventory can be obsolete and not saleable.

This is leading up to one important principle. You want as much of your assets as possible to be liquid and most of your debt to be long-term or retired. Here is how to do it:

SUPPLIERS AND ACCOUNTS PAYABLE

First, look at your suppliers and their respective accounts payable. By now, this is probably the most critical area anyway. Schedule meetings with these people on an individual basis. The goal is to encourage these suppliers to take their present debt and change it somehow. Another goal, if not the most important, is to persuade them to continue extending credit on an open account basis. And, if possible, get additional dating. Dating is a system where payment for current purchases is spread out over several months or is due sometime in the not-too-near future.

Supplier negotiations are never easy. They are complicated because your credit could be, for the most part, in jeopardy anyway. However, do not assume that your suppliers will not go along with you. You might be surprised. The important facet of this exercise is simple. If you do not ask, you will not get. Set high goals. Any concession or additional terms you get may be better than what you have now. If your goal with a supplier is to have him keep you on open account, you might ask for extended terms or dating. He may refuse that request, but he may continue to sell to you on an open account basis as a compromise.

Here is a serious hypothetical complication. You now owe a major supplier a substantial amount of money that is 120 days old. The supplier is putting pressure on you for payment. You are not on COD, but he wants you to pay previous invoices before he will ship you any more merchandise. What do you do?

That particular debt must be restructured. Here are some suggestions:

Ask your supplier's sales representative to arrange a meeting at your place between you, the credit manager, and the general manager of the supplier involved. If the supplier is owned by someone who is accessible to you, then you only need to meet with him alone.

At the meeting, show these people your operation and what you are doing to remedy the condition. Talk about the cost-saving systems you are installing. Talk about the positive changes in your business. Talk about the future and how good it looks. In other words, impress them that you are in control of your destiny. After this has been accomplished, tell them what you need from them to help you out. Ask for the moon. You may get it. In any event, whatever you get will be better than what you had.

What, specifically, could you get from this supplier? You could ask for additional terms. In other words, ask to be given another 30 or 60 days credit. Or if he is planning to put you on COD, ask that this not be done.

Another tactic is to ask your suppliers to spread out the money you owe on a payment schedule. If they agree, you can take the old accounts payable and put that amount into a note. Then, set up a payment schedule in equal monthly payments, preferably at no interest. After this arrangement has been agreed upon, ask for the first payment to be delayed 30 days. They have gone this far; they might do it if you ask. Now you are current and not 120 days past due.

As a last resort, you might want to take the approach of returning inventory in lieu of payment. This is a good way to restructure the debt if the inventory returned is slow-moving or obsolete. Do not feel badly about giving back obsolete inventory. Remember, they sold it to you in the first place. They have a better opportunity for selling it than you. Do not give back inventory that is fast moving. You will only have to go out and buy it again anyway.

Returning inventory in lieu of paying accounts payable is a good ploy, because you can get it off your books at a cost close to what you originally paid. You may have to pay a small restocking charge. The other alternative is to convert unwanted inventory by having a sale.

No matter what you arrange, make sure that you continue your relationship with the supplier. The only time you give up on a supplier is when he gives up on you. When that happens, do not give him anything. Wait until he turns you over to a collection agency or lawyer. At that time, you can negotiate for terms, or the return of merchandise, or both. You can usually get more flexibility from a lawyer or collection agency (if you are cooperative) than you can get from the supplier in the first place. Lawyers and collection agencies find negotiation a solution to conflict, whereas suppliers often do not. Of course, once it goes that far, you will never be able to buy from those suppliers again; so, before burning your bridges, make sure you categorically do not need them.

Bank payments can also be restructured. You may even be delinquent and getting pressure from the bank or finance company (this applies to lease payments on equipment also), but do not panic. They are regularly more willing to negotiate than your suppliers. After all, they really do not want to foreclose on the loan or repossess the equipment. Except for autos and certain other equipment, there is a limited market for repossessed items, so they will negotiate.

A company had equipment leases at 18% interest, payable in seven years (balloon payment). The company got behind on the payments, and the leasing company threatened repossession. The company went to the leasing company and renegotiated the deal. Here is what they got:

- One year moratorium on any payments
- Reduced interest to 12%
- Extended amortization to 15 years

Those negotiations netted the company some truly great concessions: A one year grace period with no payments; a reduction of payments from $120,000 per month to a little over $70,000 per month; a cash-flow saving of $50,000 per month, and the lease is paid in full instead of a balloon payment due in seven years.

Another organization had a fleet of leased autos and trucks. The leasing company was ready to repossess because the lease was seriously delinquent. The company renegotiated a deal where they got 50% of their fleet updated to new vehicles. They also received a considerable amount of cash from the accumulated equity, which they used to make the payments for the next three months.

CHAPTER 11

The ultimate restructuring instrument is a Chapter 11. Chapter 11 does not mean that you are out of business. Quite the contrary. Chapter 11, under the Federal Bankruptcy Act, means that you are going to reorganize and the creditors involved are forced to agree to your plan. You cannot be sued for anything that occurred before filing a Chapter 11. This applies to secured creditors as well. You cannot get evicted, nor can your assets be attached. In other words, you are fully protected from your creditors.

There are two major disadvantages of a Chapter 11. First, there is a stigma attached to bankruptcy that may cause you problems with your customers. For example, a printer who printed publications for various companies and organizations was aware of how his customers felt about reliability of supply. A notice of Chapter 11 would have frightened the customers away.

The second disadvantage is that suppliers become very cautious when doing business with a company in Chapter 11. Virtually all open account credit will dry up, and borrowing money will be very difficult as well.

Years later, these disadvantages will still haunt you. However, Chapter 11 still may be your best option, especially if there are no other alternatives available.

Chapter 11 can save the business. For example, your eventual plan could call for all unsecured debt to be frozen and set up on a three-year payout at no interest, the first year paying only 20%, the second year 30%, and the last year 50%. That last year could even be renegotiated when it becomes due. The secured creditors cannot easily foreclose, and their arrears payments could also fall into the three-year plan. The lease on your building or facilities would also fall under the same protection. You can even break a union contract in a Chapter 11 filing.

When the condition is not that severe, an arrangement with the creditors similar to a Chapter 11 can be negotiated without actually filing. Many creditors will realize that they have no choice but to go along voluntarily or be forced into compliance by a Chapter 11.

There are sensible advantages to avoiding a Chapter 11. One is that your customers will not have to be alarmed by a chapter filing because there will not be any. Another advantage is the cost. It is noticeably less expensive because you may not need an attorney. In some cities, the Credit Managers Association will do most of the work for you.

REVIEW

The main steps in restructuring the debt are:

1. Use creative methods to enhance the balance sheet.
2. Adopt a philosophy that "cash is king."
3. Convert the slow-moving inventory.
4. Get more time or terms from creditors.
5. Negotiate the return of unwanted inventory.
6. Renegotiate the bank loans.
7. Consider a Chapter 11 or some similar action.

Remember the importance of time? Now you understand why you need time to complete a turnaround. The strategies and negotiations mentioned in this chapter will require months to complete. These strategies will also get you the time you need. It follows that one gets the other. Set up a priority list of what steps you should take first. Your initial focus should render you an advantage both in cash and time; and, given a choice between the two, take time first.

Chapter 5

FINDING OTHER RESOURCES THAT ARE CASH

You are managing a distressed business. You are under pressure. "CASH IS KING," and you need to get your hands on some *quickly*. If that scenario is your reality, you must aggressively look for cash in every nook and cranny. Irrespective of what you may have already done, you do have other resources. They may not be obvious, but they are there.

Funds used *correctly* can extend the life of the business long enough to make the turnaround possible. Yet, on the other hand, a word of caution: Cash used improperly will not help you at all.

For example, a financially distressed company sold a piece of property to raise some capital. The owner, wanting some relief from the pressure, paid up all his accounts payable. He even paid the accounts payable that were not yet due. Soon thereafter, sales fell drastically, and the company suffered some large operating losses. Here is how his cash position was affected:

Because sales were generally down, there was no need to buy merchandise, and, because he did not owe any money on accounts payable, the owner was not able to raise cash by stalling payments. When the crunch came, he had a difficult time making his payroll. It was almost a disaster. When asked why he used the money the way he did, the owner replied, "Well, I didn't want the money to just sit idle in my checking account, especially while I was behind on my bills. Besides, how was I supposed to know that the economy was going to turn bad?"

His first error was believing the money would sit idle in the checking account. There were many things he could have done with the money. For starters, he could have paid only those creditors who were threatening or pressuring him. He could have used some of the money to reduce his bank debt, which would have saved the interest expense of 14%. Later, if he needed money, he could have borrowed it against his paid-down credit line. At worst, he could have put the funds in a money market account, where it could earn interest yet still be readily available.

There is a lesson to be learned from this example: Never allow yourself to run out of cash during the repair program. If you are fortunate in finding some cash, be exceptionally careful how you use it.

USING REAL ESTATE

Explore other areas that can render a substantial monetary find. You may have already discovered some of these ideas, but do not be discouraged; there may be at least one more you have not thought of yet.

Real estate is an outstanding vehicle for generating critical funds. By converting the equity held in real estate, you can use that money to save your business.

In a turnaround, selling the real estate is generally better than borrowing against it, because sold real estate brings in cash that does not have to be paid back. Look at it this way. Suppose you have $50,000 equity in a piece of real estate (other than the facilities you occupy). You have two choices. One, sell the property and put the $50,000 into your business; or two, refinance the property, pull out the equity, and put it into your business. Either way, you end up with the available $50,000. With the latter method, you now have some additional mortgage payments. This may be all right as long as the business can easily make those payments.

If the property is going up in value, then, of course, it would be wise to hold on to it. You can still unlock the equity by refinancing. If you are occupying the real estate yourself, you would be very foolish to give up the ownership, as you would gain nothing on a cash flow basis.

LIFE INSURANCE

Another often forgotten resource is your life insurance policy. The cash value that has built up happens to be an excellent source for quick funds. Sometimes this can be a huge sum of money, as in the following instance.

An office supply firm that was having financial difficulties was fully borrowed and unable to obtain another loan. A consultant told the owner that the cash value of his life insurance was about $600,000 — enough collateral to refinance the entire organization.

EQUIPMENT

Sometimes an organization has valuable machinery or equipment which could be sold or refinanced. Maybe the equipment is infrequently used and would not hurt the business if it was sold. If selling the equipment would hurt the business, then consider using it as collateral for a secured loan. It may take all the equipment or machinery as collateral to obtain the amount of money you need.

Even if you owe money on some machinery or equipment, you can still possibly pull cash out of the equity by refinancing. For example, you may have a piece of machinery worth $100,000 on today's market against which you might easily borrow $70,000. Suppose you now owe $30,000. If you refinance, you'll pull out $40,000. Most likely, your monthly payments will not change, and they may even become lower because of a better interest rate.

INVENTORY

On occasion, you can sell off some of your inventory to find more cash. The idea is to sell it at the best possible price or somewhere close to wholesale. Obviously, in order to do this in a timely way, you may have to "fire sale" some of the inventory, and, most likely, you will not get the best price. Your need for capital must be carefully weighed against the loss to determine what is an acceptable sacrifice. If the inventory in question is obsolete or slow moving, then consider that the immediate conversion money (although at a loss) is more sensible than getting full price. You may take half price and be happy you got that much.

While on the subject of inventory, that asset also has a potential for borrowing. Just as your accounts receivable, your inventory also has borrowing power. Do not ignore this possibility because you already have both your inventory and accounts receivable pledged to a bank (that is common). No matter, you still have another option:

Find yourself an asset-based lender (it could be a bank). They will usually lend you as much as 50% of your inventory and as much as 80% to 85% of your current (90 days or less) accounts receivable. Add this up for yourself. Is it more than you now have on loan? Even if you have already pledged the accounts receivable and inventory, you may still have more borrowing power if you change the method of financing.

Interestingly, not only will you get more money by changing to this type of financing, but it is a floating line of credit as well. As you buy more inventory, you can borrow more money. As you make more sales, your accounts receivable increases and so does your cash availability.

PENSION FUND

Another resource that can bring in cash is your pension fund, Keogh, or even some old IRAs. You can use this money for a short period of time without an IRS penalty. However, you might be forced to pay an early withdrawal penalty to the bank, so be careful.

Some plans allow you to borrow against the equity of your pension fund. Check this out with your plan administrator. Each plan has its own rules and opportunities.

EQUITY FINANCING

Big companies raise cash by selling stock. This method of raising money is outstanding because, theoretically, it never has to be paid back. They call this "equity financing." Supposedly, the investor will have the promise of dividends or stock value appreciation, but it is not guaranteed or even required. The main disadvantage is that you must be accountable to shareholders; and that could be a problem. Some owners do not want partners of any kind, even though they may be minority shareholders.

The advantages of equity financing can be better explained by telling you about a small company that needed money to expand. They were already heavily borrowed and getting a loan was quite impossible. The owner approached some of his key employees with a plan to allow them to become shareholders. He sold six of his key employees blocks of stock in amounts of $5,000 and raised $30,000. He still owned 95% of the company and the controlling vote, thus not giving up anything important. Later, he used the same strategy to raise more money, always keeping controlling interest.

The result was gratifying. His employees were happy because they felt they had become entrepreneurs and were now part of the organization. It did not cost the owner anything since he never paid dividends anyway.

The fringe benefit was even more rewarding. He now had several devoted, minority partners, and this arrangement caused no adverse effects. Coincidentally, a few years later, he was forced to fire one of them. Even then he was not required to cash him out. As it turned out, the other employees voluntarily bought back the shares.

REVIEW

The resources that can be converted into much needed cash are:

1. Real estate
2. Cash value of life insurance
3. Sale of equipment
4. Refinance of equipment
5. Sale of inventory
6. Refinance accounts receivable and inventory
7. Pension fund/Keogh or IRA
8. Equity financing

The event that usually triggers a turnaround is the absence of enough funds to run the business. Along with that, the traditional sources for borrowing refuse to lend any more money. When the survival of the enterprise depends on locating emergency cash, other resources must be tapped. Most likely, management has already used some, or perhaps most, of the eight resources listed above. If there is still a desperate need for additional capital, management must find more. If the organization is to survive, all stops must be pulled out, and no idea should be ignored or overlooked.

Chapter 6

MANAGING THE TURNAROUND

Running an operation is like being a juggler in a circus. There are many balls that must be kept in the air at the same time.

What seems to use up most of a manager's time? Putting out fires, correct? Are you constantly faced with one crises after another? When the typical day is over, do you feel frustrated because you cannot put your finger on anything that was really accomplished. If these are reactions to a normal environment, what about a turnaround?

When a business is sick or has severe problems, the pressure increases dramatically, and the manager is faced with responsibilities that will transcend any capable executive's ability. If typically, there is not enough time to do the managing in a normal environment, then how do you find the time to manage a turnaround? Do you work 24 hours every day straight through?

It is generally acknowledged that a CEO works an average of 50 to 60 hours per week. CEO's complain that they never seem to have enough time to do the fine tuning that they want to do in marketing, production planning, or personnel. They say those "nice-to-do" things usually suffer, but, on the whole, they get done eventually.

In a turnaround environment, a multitude of critical details can easily overwhelm a CEO. There are constant meetings and discussions. The telephone never leaves his hand. One crises after another needs his attention. In essence, the job is impossible unless the CEO changes his managerial behavior. In other words, he cannot manage the same way he did when the business was healthy.

PRIORITIES

The basic fault in any managerial style is failure to set priorities correctly. In a turnaround, that basic fault can be a disaster leading to failure.

Here is an example: There was a large printing firm that was losing about 25% on sales annually. The cash reserves were all but gone, and the company's net worth was a considerable minus figure. Suppliers would only deal with them on a cash-deposit basis. Along with that, a cash-in-advance payment was also required on routine purchases. Millions of dollars of printing presses were sitting idle, and the company's largest customer recently opened his own plant. The list of troubles go on and on. The general manager, after 29 years of service, gave up and resigned. It appeared that only one solution remained: close it down.

The owner was in deep and on the hook with personal guarantees. So, he decided to bring in another Chief Operating Officer and give it one more try. After one week on the job, the new manager came to the conclusion that virtually every facet of that operation was in distress. Every department, from production to personnel, was in trouble, and the new manager did not know where to start first. His staff drained his time with a multitude of problems. The phone never stopped ringing. At the end of his usual 14-hour day, he found himself mentally and physically exhausted. Something had to change, or this new manager would also fail.

He asked for help from a well known consultant, who specialized in turnarounds. Here is the essence of that advice:

First, do not try to solve all the problems at once. That is a mistake. Start by identifying problems and areas that require immediate attention and list them on a blackboard. Be sure to have your people involved with this exercise. This is a crucial step.

Employee interaction with the problems is imperative if the process is going to work. You can attain success with this procedure if you make it an operational program. Appoint a task force group from among your key employees. They need not be in upper-level management. They should either be supervising or running specific operations. They will become the shakers and movers. Approach these key employees individually and ask them if they would like to participate as members of the "Task Force Group." Explain the purpose of the group and how you expect them to function. Let them know how important this group is and what you believe they can accomplish. Tell them that you are hoping they will fix the problems and troubles of the organization and help the company get back on its feet again.

Schedule task force meetings on a regular basis; for example, every Monday at 3:00 pm. These meetings, especially at the beginning, may last several hours. Try to keep them under four hours. After that, people get too weary to function at their best. Do not make it a party, but do create some excitement that will make them look forward to the meetings.

In the beginning, you may want the task force to meet weekly because of the amount of repair work necessary. Later, you can schedule them biweekly or, at worst, monthly.

For the best results, you should be open and share with them the troubles of the business as you see them. Allow them to tell you what they see, even though it might be unpleasant for you. The goal is to establish two-way communication that leads to affirmative action. Remember one thing: It is through their enthusiastic labor that you can survive.

Once you and your group identify the tasks, it will become obvious that *they* will have to carry them out. If they are not solidly behind what you are trying to achieve, you will fail. Lastly, make them feel important and spend some time with them individually. The results will please you.

At the very beginning, maybe even at the first meeting, do the listing exercise previously discussed. After you and your team develop the list (which may be huge), ask the participants to articulate their feelings about specific items listed on the blackboard. Allow enough time so that everyone can have a say. You will be surprised and enlightened by their input.

You and your task force should now have a thorough understanding of the problems. Secure agreement on what, in fact, are the real attention areas. Then, and only then, can you go on to the next step.

The next step is another group exercise — to review every item listed and then number these items in the order of their importance to the company. This is a time-consuming process that may require a meeting or two all by itself. Establishing priorities by the group or committee method is the reason it will take time. Everyone will see the priorities differently. It is a natural tendency for the participants to believe those things close to their own area of influence should be the company's priorities. Your job, as the leader, is to sift through the personalities and identify what is ultimately important.

Remember, your objective is a remedial program. As the leader, you must challenge your staff's reasoning. Are the priorities correct for the best results? Is your staff in tune with the requirements of the turnaround? Is that how they came up with the priorities in the first place? If most of those answers are "no," then you, as the leader, must take the time to educate your staff and bring them up to speed.

At any time in the process you can exercise your authority and set the priorities yourself. On some issues you might have to do that. But the ideal way for this to succeed is for your people to become committed to the same things that you are committed to. When the whole team moves together, focused on the same objective, a special synergy develops. A super-heated enthusiasm also develops, and the entire team achieves what, heretofore, seemed impossible. If your staff becomes polarized, committed only to their own interests, the remedial program will suffer.

The last step in the process is to isolate the five most important priorities. They are not the easiest, but the most important. If the earlier exercise was completed properly, the five most important items should be listed on the blackboard with the numbers one through five.

Take a break at this point, but meet again within the week. Ask everyone to think about those five most important areas of concern. Let them know that the agenda of the next meeting will be the discussion of the five tasks. To make this professional, have someone who is good at taking minutes copy all the information from the blackboard. Type a summary of the meeting listing all the areas of concern organized by their priority. At the top of the list, isolate the five most important priorities so that they are clearly identified. Make it look as though you are concerned with those five alone.

At the next meeting (using the five priorities), try to establish a critical path for the company. Once you have completed the series of meetings and identified the tasks, you and your staff should now have only two types of daily activities. The first is to spend some time and energy (every day) on one or all of the five priorities. Do not spend any of your valuable time on the others. As people bring you projects, tell them that you recognize that there are, indeed, other problems to be solved. However, they are not at the top of the company's list of critical-path priorities. After you have completed the most important projects, then, and only then, spend time and energy with less critical matters.

This program is hard to do, even though it sounds easy. Your natural tendency is to get involved and spend time on any legitimate concern.

However, it is imperative that you do not spread yourself thin. Say to yourself, "No! I'm not going to spend my precious and limited time on anything that diverts me from those five priorities."

The second daily activity you and your staff should do is manage the operations. See that the systems work; monitor the activities of the employees; handle the customers; do the purchasing. Do not short-change the business by spending your limited time on solving problems that are not on the top five list.

After you have completed a priority, add another to take its place on your list. If you did your exercise correctly in the first place, the next one, number 6, should be at the top of the list. Just make sure that the added item is still as important as it was when the list was originally made or that some other item has not become more important.

When the system works correctly, some amazing results can accrue. This program was installed in a check printing company that was having some difficult times. A great deal of the difficulties were caused by extreme employee apathy and discord. Management had a particular style that did not encourage employee participation, and, over the years, the lower levels of supervision degenerated to a destructive state. Even though most of the people had the capacity, they were not in tune with the objective of the business. Each supervisor managed his own little fiefdom with little concern for the big picture.

A task force group was installed, and a series of meetings took place similar to what has been described in this chapter. They identified more than 100 items for remedial action. Within 45 days, more than 50 items had been completed and another five were near completion. By the end of three months, 80 items were completed and the organization was greatly improved. Moreover, a new communication among supervisors had developed. Managers were no longer working independently of each other. A teamwork ethic had developed.

As a part of the turnaround, a large satellite plant had to be consolidated with the main factory. The concern was that a major disruption in service could badly damage the firm. Customers would not tolerate a return to the days when service and quality were marginal. Because of the task force group, the consolidation was accomplished without missing a stroke. The team pulled together with an astonishing passion for excellence. A multitude of individual time-sensitive tasks were accomplished accurately and on time. The group created a giant Gantt chart, and everyone did his share to make sure they were on schedule.

The result was a tremendous financial savings for the company.

REVIEW

The basic procedures for managing the turnaround are:

1. Know your time limitations (your staff's also).
2. List all the problems and projects.
3. Number them by importance.
4. Do not try to solve all the problems at once.
5. Take on only the top five as a priority.
6. Say "no" to other concerns, however legitimate.
7. Manage operations without neglecting the day-to-day work.

Do not ever put anything new on a full plate. Do not start new projects until you finish the ones you have already begun. Remember, your time is not an unlimited resource. Do not let yourself get bogged down to a point where you cannot function or not in control of your own activities. Make sure that your staff understands this as well. Be gracious with people, but ruthless with time.

PART THREE

THE SEVEN ELEMENTS

Chapter 7

PERSONNEL EFFECTIVENESS

It is often said that good employees are the most valuable asset of a business. Repairing the ills of a deteriorating business makes this axiom even more true. Yet, at the same time, it must be recognized that many of the company's problems are also labor intensive. In other words, to what degree do the employees share in the faults?

If the employees take their share of glory in a healthy and successful company, then they must also share some responsibility when the business becomes unhealthy. After all, sick organizations do not happen by themselves. Leadership and employees can make or break a business. In turnarounds, the employees may, in fact, be responsible for breaking the business.

How do your employees feel about what is going on right now? Regardless of what you think, they know the company is in trouble. To what extent may still be unknown, but they are aware of more than you imagine. If asked, they will not claim responsibility because they do not believe they are at fault. They perceive that they are clean. If anything, they are blaming you. If not you, then your upper-level management team. Meanwhile, your management team is blaming everyone but themselves. They may say that it is your fault because you have tied their hands or given them poor direction.

On the positive side, employees generally want to see the company become well again. It is not in their best interests to follow the business into bankruptcy. If approached properly, they will do just about anything to help. The difficult part is convincing them that many of the ills are caused by their own apathy or political games.

There is always a group of hard-core bureaucrats that view their fiefdom as inviolate. Only they know what is best. They use political and officious methods to maintain their domination over certain operations. They are empire builders and political hard ballers. They have survived over time by confusing the issues and getting rid of anyone who opposes them. They are dangerous and will work at odds with you and your staff in any remedial program. Their priorities are self-centered and, to make matters even more difficult, they do not recognize their own motives. They may even appear to be conscientious. If you do not know who these people are, here are some clues as to how to find them:

The most obvious clue is their defensiveness. They are constantly trying to prove they are right and others are wrong. They are very quick to point out the mistakes and errors of everyone else. They hold a strong power base and have many allies, because most people like to associate themselves with powerful people, especially the survivors. They verbalize problems with the *we can't* approach instead of the *we can* approach. They tend to either "suck-up" to you or totally ignore your wishes. In either case, the response is always in the extreme. Many times they will tell you how valuable they are to the company and may even threaten to resign.

You must weed these people out — the sooner the better. You may find yourself hesitant. To some extent, it is because they have made themselves hard to replace. It is the nature of their long-term behavior. They have made themselves important to your business, and they control vital operations. Because of their basic insecurity, they have not developed a strong replacement potential from within the ranks. So, letting them go presents a problem. If you allow procrastination to slow down your efforts to replace them, you will, most likely, never do it. Waiting only puts off the inevitable.

ORGANIZATIONAL ANALYSIS

Irrespective of who is at fault, it is, however, a good exercise to find out what or who caused the dilemma in the first place. This discovery process is called an "Organizational Analysis."

This discovery process determines organizational responsibilities, who reports to whom, who should be gotten rid of, and who should be promoted. Moreover, you need to know who you can count on for that extra effort. You need to ferret out excess baggage in the ranks of the employees, and to vigorously carry out terminations where necessary.

Contrary to the belief of present management, there is always fat in the employee ranks. This is especially true in financially distressed organizations. As a rule of thumb, you can always eliminate 10% of the work force. When sales are decreasing, you can and must cut even more. Just make sure that you are cutting redundant personnel and not critical operations. Make sure that likable personnel do not survive the hard-working and needed individuals. Review every termination recommendation twice, and do it personally.

Owners often think they know what is going on. They make assumptions about how employees behave. They believe they know their people well. They even know their limitations. To some extent, this is true, but then why do the owners allow certain situations to exist? For example:

An owner had to replace one of his division managers due to illness. He promoted the division manager's assistant to take over. He knew the assistant very well since he had worked for the company for more than 15 years in various capacities. Besides, the assistant was genuinely a loyal employee and a nice guy to boot. He never argued with anyone, nor had he become political. Everyone loved him. The owner knew this fellow was not dynamic or aggressive and was somewhat weak in certain skills. But, all in all, the owner felt he was a good choice.

It took less than two years for the division to deteriorate to a point of embarrassment. Every fundamental control and system was in shambles. Sales people ran wild. They even controlled the pricing. Invoices were lost, and money was never collected. Costs went out of sight. You name it, and it was wrong. Losses for the division were astonishing. They were losing $3 million on $12 million in sales.

Where was the owner? Everyone speculated that he must have known what was going on. But if that were true, how could he let it continue? To this day the owner does not believe that he made a mistake. He still does not understand why things came out the way they did. As an excuse, he even blamed the mess on the economy. That was hard to do since their sales increased 20% in that two-year period.

It is obvious to any outsider analyzing the situation. The owner lost control of the details. He left it to his employees. Unfortunately, he gave them little leadership and direction. He said he trusted them, and his trust was not misplaced. The owner was right, they were honest and loyal. They just did not know what was expected of them. Moreover, they could not get any help.

This problem was not relegated to just this one division of the company. Similar employee problems permeated the entire company—

from the shipping department to the computer room; from the sales force to the accounting department; from the warehouse to the executive office. People-wise, everything was in serious trouble. Employees did exactly what they thought was important. The big picture was never made clear. Department heads had their own agenda. Nothing was coordinated, and the company suffered on a global basis. The state of the business was in such disrepair that the bank which financed the equipment insisted that new management be brought in to run the operation.

So, the owner was forced to hire new management. The solutions to the company's distress were available to the new management. However, because the culture of the company was so ingrained and established, it took years to straighten out.

Start your organizational analysis by preparing an organizational chart. This is similar to building a pyramid. Start at the top with the Chief Executive Officer or Chief Operating Officer. Under him, list horizontally the people who report directly to him. Under them, list horizontally (on the next level) the people who report to them, and so forth. This chart will clarify who reports to whom as well as reinforce the employee's own perception of the reporting order.

SUPERVISION

Over the history of mankind, the discovery and use of defined people supervision has always amazed us with outstanding results. When Moses left Egypt, it took him 40 years of wandering to unearth the power of supervision. It took him 40 years to cross a very small piece of land, but when he installed a system of supervision, the Jews met their goal in just a short time. The system was actually quite basic and conformed closely to our common decimal system of mathematics. Moses appointed a leader to be in charge of 10 men, and a leader to be in charge of 10 leaders. This progression went on and on until everyone had some responsibility and reported to someone. As a leader of 10 men died, he was replaced from within his own cadre.

The Roman army used a remarkably similar system of officers called Centurions (a derivative of the word Century, meaning 100). In recent history, the United States military forces won battles in the field because their supervision system was broken down to its most basic level. As non-commissioned and commissioned officers got killed, they were easily replaced from within their own ranks. Each member was trained to move up one position, a modest jump. Japanese businesses learned this lesson well. Hypothetically, a Japanese worker even supervises himself.

The organization chart plots your supervision system. That is why you must prepare this road map. When you have completed this task, ask yourself these questions:

1. How many people report to the CEO? Theoretically, no more than five or six should report to him; otherwise, he may lose his effectiveness as a manager. Suppose your chart shows eight people reporting to the CEO, what now? Take the time to redesign or retitle the functions of some people so that the CEO has as few people as possible reporting to him. Can some of them report to someone else?

2. How is the second level structured? Who is on that level? They should be the best you have. The second level is the most important in the organizational structure. This is the department head level—the CEO's team. This is the level where the leadership originates. They support the entire organization. Without good, strong people in those spots, the CEO cannot function. Because of their importance, careful thought and effort should be devoted to their selection.

This tier in the management structure should have a vice president or department head at these main functions:

- Accounting/office/bookkeeping/computer
- Production/warehouse/operations/purchasing
- Sales/marketing/order desk/customer service

Notice, there are only three areas of responsibility that make up the entire operation. By necessity, it may be more desirable to make it five or six by separating the sales and marketing functions, the accounting and office functions, or the production and operations functions. On the following page is a chart of a company with a five-person executive team.

ORGANIZATION CHART

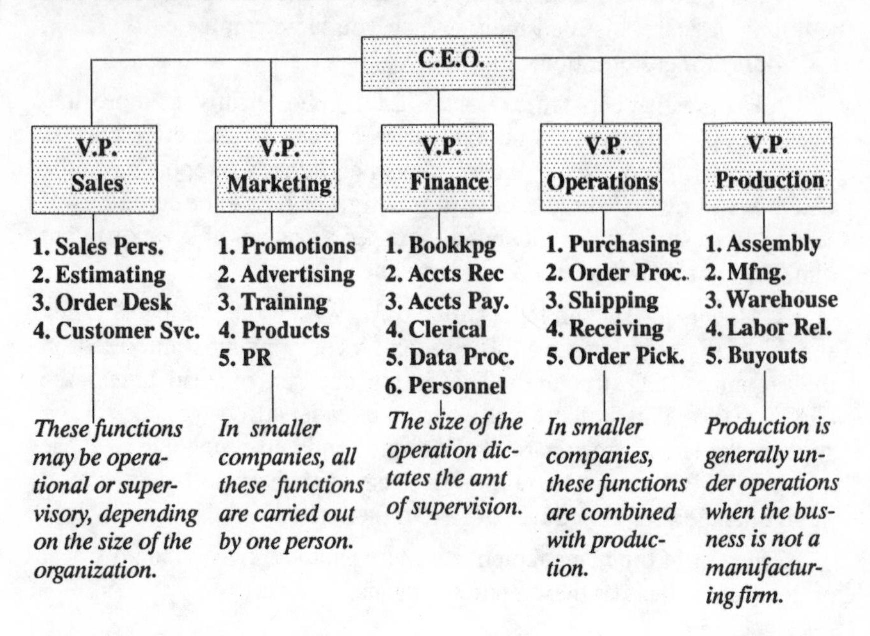

The size of the organization dictates the amount of management at the lower levels. For example, under manufacturing, there may be four assembly departments. It would be desirable to have some type of supervision for each department, all reporting to the manufacturing manager.

Breaking down supervisory functions to their lowest level is a more appropriate style in today's working environment. You may be thinking, "all chiefs and no Indians?" It does appear that way. One would think that everybody stands around and directs others, but that is not really the case. Everyone in management, or, for that matter, everyone in supervision, has specific operational duties — even the CEO. Supervisors may actually be the workers as well. Lead people devote most of their time to defined operational functions, so that, in reality, everyone is working, and, at the same time, they have some supervisory responsibilities. The higher up the ladder, the more time they spend supervising. The lower their supervisory level, the more time they spend doing the work.

Having responsible supervision at all levels leads to a better com munication system, both upwards and downwards. Moreover, supervision is immediately accessible to their subordinates. That accessibility is the key to smooth and successful operations.

WEEDING PROCESS

There is one more task that is difficult, and possibly distasteful, but important and necessary. You must get rid of nonfunctional and redundant personnel, even though they may have been with you a long time. If you do not scale down the personnel numbers, it will hamper your ability to save the company. As difficult as it may be, you must put the survival of the company above your personal feelings. Survival of the whole takes precedence over any individual.

There are some simple methods for a planned reduction of employees. The worst method is to not replace anyone that leaves. In the real world, this often happens because it is easy to reduce people that way; no one has to be fired.

Unfortunately, this is wrong. A planned reduction cannot be accomplished on a hit-or-miss basis. People that leave are not necessarily redundant. They may be key employees. Shuffling people around can work sometimes, but it is rare. Usually, incompetent employees end up in responsible positions. Planned reductions are exactly that — planned.

You must start at the top and decide who you can get rid of without damaging the firm. The top is an ideal place to begin, because that is the place to find the larger salaries. One executive salary may be worth five or six workers. Once the top tier has been culled down, invite the remaining department heads or surviving managers to a planning session, the object of which is to discuss and originate a comprehensive employee reduction plan. Each manager decides who will remain and how the work will get accomplished with a reduced staff.

Before putting into action any plan, make sure your managers use proper reasoning in their selection. You do not want them to show favoritism to those employees who are friends.

You are the one who must set the reduction goal. The numbers should be developed mathematically from the accounting department, based on bottom-line mentality. You know the dollars that must be cut, and this can then be translated into numbers of people. Be firm in this action because everyone will be against personnel eliminations.

REVIEW

The principles of personnel effectiveness are:

1. Recognize the importance of good people.
2. Analyze the management structure.
3. Make a company organizational chart.
4. Restructure the management reporting flow.
5. Make sure managers are accessible to their subordinates.
6. Limit the amount of people reporting to any one person.
7. Reduce numbers by at least 10%.

Without the cooperation of the rank and file employees, a turnaround is almost impossible. With their support and enthusiasm, a repair program can be notably easier. Moreover, it can be a gratifying experience.

Chapter 8

MANAGING ORGANIZATIONAL SYSTEMS

Statistical findings show that businesses that go bankrupt have common ailments. One of those common ailments is *poor business records*. In addition to poor records, they show that virtually every control or procedure has deteriorated or even disappeared.

To establish a common language, these procedures and controls are called "systems."

Every organization has its own particular way of doing things. Systems evolve over a long period of time to accommodate the needs of the business. There is no universal standard procedure or system list available. Even well-managed companies have different systems. Therefore, you will not get any magic answers here. What you will get is a check list. With this check list, you can review your own operation and possibly install some new systems.

THE COMPUTER SOLUTION

Many existing systems radically change when you install a new computer. Moreover, managers work very hard to make the new computer work by taking short cuts with manual controls. Herein lies the answer to why certain things occur. When mistakes are examined in retrospect, you wonder why someone did not say something about what was going on. They should have, but they did not because everyone wants the computer.

A manufacturing firm replaced its old tried and dependable accounting system with a new computer. The computer was installed mainly to handle inventory. However, it also had an order entry system attached to it. Some years later, the owner inadvertently discovered that orders could be entered, manufactured, and shipped without ever being billed, especially if the paperwork somehow got misplaced after shipping. To his chagrin, they had done away with the master log of invoices when they installed the new computer. There was no procedure in place that said, "If we ship something, we must bill something." Ironically, the problem was discovered during a possible embezzlement investigation.

Buying a computer for your business will not solve your financial troubles, your system inadequacies, or any other important problems you might have. The computer is only a tool, not a panacea. Just as a typewriter is better and faster than handwriting letters, a computer is better than some manual systems, because it may be faster and provide more information. Like anything else, each procedure must stand on its own.

A manual system may be more efficient than a computer for some procedures. Do not replace it solely because you bought a computer and feel compelled to put everything possible on it.

For example, there was a large graphics firm that was using a sophisticated computer for accounts payable. Things were always a mess. They made double payments, missed discounts, and made a host of other mistakes. It was impossible to reconcile any vendor complaint about a payment. They had four people in the department, and not one of them was in control. When new management took over, they discovered the problem was with the computer.

As a side note, the computer was functioning extremely well doing other tasks. Only the accounts payable was a mess. The new management installed a One-Write (manual system) accounting system for the accounts payable. In one month they had everything in order. They could look at any vendor ledger card and tell instantly what they owed and when it was due. Reconciliations were handled over the phone. Cash discounts were never missed, and, of course, not one double payment was ever made again. To top it off, they reduced the department staff to just one part-time high school student.

Look at it this way. A computer is a tool, like a knife. It could be used to slice a piece of bread, or, if turned against you, it could take your life. Computers are tools with limitations. Do not install them where they do not belong. As a general rule, do not install a computer system where no other system existed before.

SYSTEMS CHECK LIST

In examining your systems, let's start with a comprehensive check list and the questions you should ask about each system:

ORDER ENTRY

1. Are all invoices accounted for?
2. Do your business forms do it all with no other repetitive forms?
3. Does your order entry form become the billing form?
4. Is the price verified? What about the math?
5. Do you have a back log system?

Nothing happens until a sale is made. Order entry is the beginning of the process for handling that sale. Mess it up here, and it stays messed up. The objective is smooth paperwork flow, and accounting control. Nothing less than perfection should be tolerated here.

PRODUCTION

1. Is the estimate you priced the same as the job you got?
2. Is your cost system accurate? Do you have one?
3. Do you look at every job that lost money or came in over budget?
4. Do you have an efficient scheduling system?

More money is lost in production than anywhere else. Running a loose system here can be costly. Knowing your cost is an important prerequisite to proper pricing. Your being competitive or profitable is predicated on what happens in your production department.

(Continued)

WAREHOUSE AND SHIPPING

1. Do you have an inventory system? Can you prevent an out-of-balance inventory? (Meaning 80% of your sales is for 20% of your inventory)

2. Do you have a system to prevent inventory from mysteriously disappearing?

3. Can anyone go into the warehouse and easily take merchandise to fill an order? (Namely your salespeople)

4. Does anyone double check what the shippers ship out?

5. Are receiving and shipping two separate functions?

Imbalanced inventories can ruin any business. Poor systems can lead to poor purchasing and poor purchasing can lead to obsolete inventory. Shipping is an open window, where anything can disappear through it.

BILLING AND CREDIT

1. Does your system make sure you bill everything shipped?

2. Do you check to see if the customer has a past due balance before you ship? Do you check credit at all?

3. If a customer will not pay, can you always show proof of delivery? Do you ask for purchase orders?

4. Can you quickly tell how much a customer owes you?

5. Do you send out invoices as soon as you ship?

What good is selling the merchandise if you don't receive the money? After all, why are you in business in the first place? Money is so costly you cannot afford to be lenient or sloppy in handling this area of your business.

ACCOUNTS RECEIVABLE

1. Do you send monthly statements to past due accounts?

(Continued)

2. Do you get an accounts receivable aging report?

3. Do you separate the billing function from the collection function?

4. Do you send out statements as close as possible to the first of every month?

Too much money is tied up in receivables. The closer to cash the better the system. You cannot spend accounts receivable. You have to collect the money first. That should be one of your major concerns.

COMMISSIONS

1. Do you pay commissions when the customer pays?

2. Do you get a sold order backlog report for all your sales men on draw?

3. Do you still pay commission when a customer is slow paying or more than 120 days past due?

4. Do you get a monthly draw deficit report? Does it relate to sales made or commissions due?

Poor handling of commissions can lead to unhappy salespeople. Inaccuracy here can cause damage to your sales efforts. A tight ship builds trust.

ACCOUNTS PAYABLE

1. Do you use purchase orders?

2. Are the purchasing and payable functions separated?

3. Does someone match up the PO, the receiver, and the invoice before you write a check?

4. Do you have a system that lets you know when cash discounts are due?

5. Can you tell what you owe a vendor at any particular

(Continued)

time? Can you tell what you paid and when you paid it?

6. Do you sign all checks? Do you see the paperwork at the same time?

Poor purchasing habits can be very costly. Aside from that, a loose system invites theft.

PAYROLL

1. Do all employees fill out time cards?

2. Does someone verify hours if you don't have a clock?

3. Are your reports filled out accurately and timely?

4. Do you sign payroll checks? If not, do you see them?

The laws governing employees are complicated and different from state to state and for the federal government. Errors in this area can cause legal grief and extensive fines.

INCOME STATEMENTS

1. Do you get them as close to the end of each month as possible?

2. Do they break out sales by category? Expenses by selling and G & A? Are other expenses separated by cost center?

3. When you get the statements, do you go over every item with your management team or accountant?

4. Do you compare percentages with previous years?

5. How often do you take a physical inventory to verify the figures on the statement?

6. Do you use the statements as a tool?

Income statements are the report cards of the operation. If your management team is effective, you will get high marks in the form of profits. Burying your head in the sand does not eliminate losses.

Quick response ability is paramount if you are going to reverse undesirable trends.

There were more than 54 questions in the preceding check list. How many of them could you answer? How many of them could you answer with confidence, knowing that you have that item under control? How many of the questions suggest to you the possibility for change or areas for your special attention?

The purpose of the check list is to force you to open your eyes to the systems inadequacy of your business. You might ask, "How do I fix these things?" The answer is simple. You must get help from the outside. There are several sources that you can use. You can call upon your CPA or accountant. Most accountants know systems extremely well. Another source of expertise is the people who sell these systems, such as business forms salespeople, One-Write systems salespeople, and inventory control systems salespeople. Some computer salespeople also know systems, but, generally, they do not have the type of hands-on knowledge you will require. Remember this important caveat: In a great many cases, a fine manual system or new business form will do the job as well as a new computer.

REVIEW

To manage organizational systems:

1. Businesses that go broke generally have poor systems.
2. Computers are not a panacea.
3. Make sure manual systems work first before installing a computer.
4. Be able to answer all questions on the check list.
5. Make systems a priority.

The better your systems, the better your chances of installing a successful remedial program. But, very honestly, if you are having difficulties now, most likely your systems need a great amount of work. In that case, this should become your top priority. You would be surprised how well you will sleep at night knowing that you have installed the controls and procedures necessary to have a smoothly running operation.

Chapter 9

EFFECTIVE TOOLS FOR INCREASING GROSS MARGINS

To determine what your gross margin percentage is, or, as some people call it, gross profit, you must take your cost and divide that by your selling price. This will give you your cost-of-goods-sold percentage (C/SP=CGS%).

Example:

Cost = $200

Selling price = $300

Divide 200 by 300 = .666

Now you have the cost-of-goods-sold percentage of 66.6%. To arrive at your gross margin/profit percentage, you must subtract the 66.6% from 100%. The difference is 33.3%, your gross margin/profit percentage.

There is another way of calculating the gross margin percentage. Take your selling price and subtract the cost. The balance is your profit. Then divide your profit by your selling price and you will arrive at the gross margin percentage ([SP-C]/ SP= GM%).

Example:

Selling price = $300

Cost = $200

Subtract 300 - 200 = 100

Divide 100 by 300 = .333 (33.3%)

These calculations are used to determine the percentage when you know your cost and selling price. Use the next formula to figure out what the selling price should be when you know your cost and the desired margin percentage. You can do this by first deciding what gross margin you want to achieve. For this illustration, use the 33.3% in the examples. Take your cost and divide it by the reciprocal of the desired margin (the reciprocal of 33.3 is 66.6). Dividing the cost by that figure will give you a selling price (C/[1000-DM]= SP).

Example:

Cost = $200

Desired margin 33.3%

Subtract .333 from 1.000 = .666 (the reciprocal)

Divide 200 by .666 = 300. The selling price is $300.

PRODUCT ANALYSIS

You need to know how to analyze these margins and how they are associated with what you may be faced with. The financial statements should give you some basics by giving you the calculation of the margin percentage on the whole. Should your statements not have the format which shows percentages, you must change to one that does. This is very important. In the meantime, have someone calculate those percentages and write them next to the appropriate numbers. It may not be categorized by product line. In other words, the percentage on your statement is a mix or an average margin. Therefore, the first thing you will have to do is separate the figures by product category.

Ask your CPA, bookkeeper, or accountant to give you a product analysis by gross margin. You may hear that it cannot be done because you never kept records that way. Be tenacious, and do not give up. This information is important. If your bookkeeper or accountant says he absolutely cannot give you this information, then ask him to examine the invoices for a one-month period and put it together that way. True, it will only be for one month, and it may be inaccurate because it is not a long enough sample. However, it is better than nothing.

Once you have this information, examine where you make money and where you do not make money. If your firm is similar to most businesses, then the 80/20 rule will apply. Most likely you will find that you have several products that lose money or, at best, make only a small profit. The question is: Can you get rid of those unprofitable sales without hurting the business?

Every enterprise, at one time or another, needs some lower margin sales to help cover the overhead. If it is only a one-time deal, that requires little or no resources to handle, then why not? On the other hand, if the sale requires a great deal of expense and investment or overhead, then, perhaps, you would be better off without those marginal orders. Too many unprofitable sales will kill a business. These so-called add-on sales end up requiring just as much, if not more, attention than the profitable sales. When it reaches that point, the law of diminishing returns becomes active.

SALES / PRICE RELATIONSHIP

An enjoyable way to rid yourself of unprofitable sales is to raise prices. Yes, you will lose some sales. But not as many as you might suspect. It may surprise you how customers will continue to buy from you even at the higher price.

When you raise prices, two things happen that will work for you. First, you might get rid of those unprofitable sales or customers, thereby reducing your overhead or investment to some degree. The other benefit you will receive is more profit on those that remain.

Here are some sample numbers that demonstrate the theoretical underpinning of this strategy:

Sales are $100,000 at an overall gross margin of 28% (too low to operate profitably). Twenty thousand dollars of those sales are at 16% margin, and the balance at 31%. Suppose you had a 10% price increase on that $20,000 of marginal sales? As a result of that increase, some marginally profitable customers, who mainly buy with a price consideration in mind, stopped buying from you. A 10% price increase may result in a loss of 10% to 20% of sales. Suppose the maximum of 20% quit buying. This leaves a balance of $16,000.

Now add the 10% price increase to that figure. The net sales will increase to $17,600 at a 26% gross margin. Combining that with the $80,000 at 31%, you now have a new, over-all average gross margin of approximately 30.1% on sales of $97,600. The total net profit jumped from $28,000 to $29,376. Real sales went down $2,400, and profits increased $1,376. Because sales decreased slightly, there was less inventory used, less shipping involved, less purchasing done, and less sales effort applied. In other words, it probably cost fewer dollars to operate.

Suppose you put a flat 10% price increase on everything. Using the same assumptions, here is the net effect: Sales will decrease to $88,000. Total gross margins will increase to 38%, resulting in a new net profit of

$33,440. Besides that, operating expenses will also decrease somewhat.

Be careful with this method of increasing margins. There is a degree of danger. There is a point where you will become the beneficiary of accelerated sales decreases caused by excessive price increases. It all depends on the competitive environment. An increase of 5% would probably not have any effect on sales, whereas 25% might cause a 50% decrease in sales.

In too many cases, the sales force controls pricing. Any decision concerning price should be left exclusively to the owner or general manager. Salespeople will tell you that you cannot raise prices. They will try to intimidate you and say that they will lose business.

Salespeople normally want the lowest prices. It is no wonder why they try to control the pricing policy. Unabated, this could become dangerous. A few years ago there was an office supply company that was going through some tough times. They were losing somewhere in the neighborhood of 9% on sales annually. Through intimidation, the salesmanager of the firm had upper management convinced that raising prices to any degree would lose a considerable amount of business. The salesmanager was so powerful that management always buckled under. Management tried to stop the losses by using other means. Everything failed, yet the salesmanager and his salespeople still maintained that price increases were out of the question. The situation deteriorated to a degree where they were selling some products below cost using the justification that it was absolutely necessary to maintain other sales.

The company eventually went under. The salesmanager and his salespeople went to work for the competition. It was there they learned that their prices had been much too low. Their new employers insisted on pricing that made sense. The salespeople had no choice but to go along. Interestingly enough, not one customer was lost as a result of higher prices. With 20/20 hindsight, the underpriced company would still be in business today.

The point is this: salespeople will always tell you that price is the most important element of the sale. They will tell you that you will lose customers if you raise prices. They will aggressively show you sales opportunities that were lost, putting the blame on current pricing. They will say, "Just think how many others we'll lose if we raise our prices!" In essence, they will do their utmost to stop you from considering price increases as a reasonable option to solving your financial problems.

You have to tune this out. Sometimes price increases are the best way to solve the financial dilemma. Price relates directly to gross margins. If gross margins seem to be heading downward in a decreasing trend, then reverse the trend, even if it suggests changing prices.

LOOK AT COSTS

Another element that affects the gross margins is the way you purchase or produce the product (or service) that you sell. The price of the product is only one element of the gross margin calculation. The other element is the cost of the product. This is another place where management has some control.

When financial trouble rears its ugly head, often there are supplier difficulties as well. It usually follows that there is not enough money to pay the bills. Vendors become reluctant to extend credit. Moreover, they may not want to give you the best price. These vendor attitudes can make it difficult for you to improve the company's gross margins through cost reduction.

Careful negotiations must take place in order to accomplish cost-reduction objectives. The best approach may be to involve your vendors. Make them a part of the problem and the solution as well. The one ace-in-the-hole that you have is the competitive nature of your industry. Your vendors do not want to lose your volume. It will amaze you to see how much they will help you, especially if you will communicate openly with them. Under no circumstances tell them something that will scare them into an ultraconservative credit policy. Always paint a bright future. Do not give them financial statements that show losses. Instead, show them budgets, forecasts, and projections.

Consider joining a buying cooperative. A great many industries have established them on a broad basis. If your industry does not have any existing buying groups, why not start one? Try calling some of your friendly competitors and tell them about your idea of pooling your orders with certain vendors. A group can be easily started once everyone sees how the price can dramatically improve with larger quantity purchases.

Here is another strategy. Increase your purchases with new vendors. Let some other vendors compete for your business. Get the word out that you are willing to talk with other suppliers. Tell them there are no more favored vendors and that you are willing to try someone new, provided the terms and prices are better than your present source.

Two important things will happen when you do this. To begin with, you will get better prices. You will also get a broader base of credit, thereby helping your cash flow. (More about that in the next chapter.) The second thing that will happen is a most interesting phenomenon. Your existing vendors will feel the pressure, and they will try to give you a better deal as well. They really do not want to lose you as a customer, so they will try to eliminate competition by giving you what you want.

REVIEW

These are the five areas to review:

1. Learn how to calculate margins and figure pricing.
2. Break down sales by category so that you can determine the losers and winners.
3. Try to eliminate lower margin sales.
4. Consider raising prices.
5. Try to purchase better.

In almost every instance of financial failure, the post-mortem analysts usually verify that the profit margins of the enterprise were not great enough to support the burden of the day-to-day operational expenses. Many remedial programs only focus on reducing expenses, while the margins slip away rapidly. Do not be afraid to deal with the margins. They may be a lot easier to correct than you think.

Chapter 10

BASIC PRINCIPLES OF EFFECTIVE CASH FLOW CONTROL

Effective cash flow management is a vital tool in managing the normal up and down cycles experienced during a company's life span, so much so that the accounting profession has paid particular attention to how money flows through a business by adopting a cash flow statement as a part of the financial presentation.

On occasion you may need to borrow money from a bank. Before lending you money, they will probably ask many questions associated with your cash flow effectiveness. There is a legitimate reason for this concern. Even though your firm makes a profit, it still may not be able to repay a bank loan. It all depends how the cash flows through the operation and how that cash is applied. That is why banks need information about your accounts receivable aging, the number of days in receivables, and the number of inventory turns. These are indications of how you manage the cash. These topics will be addressed in this chapter as well as what precisely influences cash flow, and we will also correct some common misconceptions. But first, a little more about the importance of cash.

Most specialists involved with repairing a company behave as though cash is the most important element. They say, "Irrespective of what happens, never run out of cash!"

Of course, that is much easier said than done, especially in a financially troubled environment. That does not necessarily mean that a person cannot have a significant effect on the cash flow. Constructive activity in this area can be effective.

SALES

Most people would automatically say that sales generate cash. But unless those sales are cash sales, they do not. In fact, it is just the opposite; sales use cash. The greater the sales increase, the more you need cash to support those sales.

In reality, cash receipts from accounts receivable, a result of sales, create cash. That does not necessarily mean "profitable sales." Money flows irrespective of profits or losses. Incoming money relates directly to cash sales, cash receipts from accounts receivable payments, and other cash-generating transactions.

Some types of losses can generate a positive cash flow; one such loss is depreciation. Depreciation is an expense that reduces profits, yet does not reduce cash. Depreciation expense is not paid to anyone and does not require money. At the same time, it does reduce the tax liability because it is an expense. Unfortunately, a financially troubled business is not usually concerned with paying income taxes unless you can apply for a refund from prior years. Ask your accountant about that possibility.

A couple of other ways to increase cash flow is to increase accounts payable (by paying more slowly) and to reduce inventory (by increasing inventory turns). Also, there is the strategy of converting short-term debt to long-term debt. (This was discussed in Chapter 4.)

CASH ANALYSIS

Once it becomes clear why good cash flow is important, you must now learn how to control it. Start this by understanding what is currently happening to your cash flow. You can do this by asking your accountant to give you a cash flow analysis. A cash flow analysis will document the sources and uses of the money. The categories in this analysis might be as follows:

SOURCES OF FUNDS

- Cash sales
- Payments on accounts receivable
- Payments on notes receivable
- Proceeds from loans

- Proceeds from the sale of assets
- Cash rebates offered by suppliers
- Refunds and reimbursements
- Miscellaneous cash receipts

USES OF FUNDS

- Accounts payable
- Operating expenses (rent, utilities, etc.)
- Payroll
- Selling expenses
- General and administrative expense
- Taxes
- Notes

Along with the analysis, you will need a month by month cash flow forecast. The following sample is for you to study:

CASH FLOW PROJECTION

ITEM	JAN	FEB	MAR	APR	MAY
Beginning Cash	**$ 9,000.**	**$ 6,800.**	**$11,100.**	**$ 9,400.**	**$13,600.**
Cash inflows :					
A/R receipts	**38,000.**	**33,500.**	**44,000.**	**6,000.**	**31,000.**
Cash sales	**6,000.**	**5,000.**	**9,000.**	**5,500.**	**4,500.**
Sale of assets	**0**	**0**	**0**	**12,000.**	**0**
Bank loan	**0**	**10,000.**	**0**	**0**	**0**
Misc.	**1,000.**	**1,000.**	**1,000.**	**1,000.**	**1,000.**
Cash outlays:					
G & A expense	**3,600.**	**3,600.**	**3,600.**	**3,600.**	**3,600.**
Selling expense	**3,200.**	**3,100.**	**3,700.**	**3,150.**	**2,900.**

ITEM	JAN	FEB	MAR	APR	MAY
Payroll	**$ 7,600.**	**$ 7,600.**	**$ 7,600.**	**$ 7,600.**	**$ 7,600.**
Accounts payable	**27,600.**	**24,600.**	**34,800.**	**27,700.**	**26,200.**
Taxes	**1,000.**	**1,000.**	**1,000.**	**1,000.**	**1,000.**
Notes	**800.**	**800.**	**1,600.**	**1,600.**	**1,600.**
Rent	**2,500.**	**2,500.**	**2,500.**	**2,500.**	**2,500.**
Utilities	**900.**	**900.**	**900.**	**900.**	**900.**
Misc.	**0**	**1,100.**	**0**	**2,250.**	**0**
Cash balance	**6,800.**	**11,100.**	**9,400.**	**13,600.**	**3,800.**

This illustration is a simple cash flow forecast that shows where the money comes from and where it goes. The sample work sheet is different from a typical income statement because this sample reflects a cash basis report without considering accruals. In other words, your financial statement takes into consideration the money that you owe as well as the money that you spent. Because you are dealing with cash flow only, you will not address accruals.

To start managing the cash, first examine the money inflows. Where do they come from? Generally, accounts receivable is one of the most important sources. Payments from accounts receivable are, by far, the largest source, and, fortunately, you can increase those inflows. Here is how:

ACCOUNTS RECEIVABLE

Start by preparing an accounts receivable aging. An aging is a report that records every customer that owes you money and how long they have owed it. To obtain this type of report, you must analyze your customer ledger cards, one by one. Then, prepare a work sheet that will look something like the one below:

CUSTOMER	TOTAL	CURRENT	30	60	90	OVER
Albert	**$ 944.10**	**$0**	**$ 944.10**	**$0**	**$0**	**$0**
Allison	**1,166.85**	**311.25**	**440.69**	**210.80**	**204.11**	**0**
Bryce	**2,111.50**	**2,111.50**	**0**	**0**	**0**	**0**
Cox	**88.50**	**0**	**0**	**0**	**88.50**	**0**
Colby	**544.39**	**18.90**	**33.89**	**491.60**	**0**	**0**
Dobbs	**109.43**	**12.55**	**0**	**0**	**0**	**96.88**

A careful analysis of this aging report will reveal some interesting information. For example, why was Dobbs issued credit last month when he had not paid an invoice that was more than 120 days old? By setting up a system to check credit first, you can eliminate these unnecessary capital drains. Moreover, you could have used Dobbs' new purchase as a lever to collect the past due money. When Dobbs placed his order, he should have been told that his order could not be shipped because he still owes on an old invoice. Very often, the delinquent invoice will be paid. Dobbs has no choice but to pay you, or he receives no merchandise. If by chance, you are his only source, then just maybe he will be forced to pay you. In any respect, you are the one in control.

Just suppose it was possible to collect all those accounts receivable that are 60 days or more. In the previous illustration, that would amount to $1,091.89—22% of the total. Imagine what you could do if you instantly collected 22% of your accounts receivable.

Your accounts receivable collections may be vulnerable if you do not have a good system in place to control this very important part of your firm's operation. By the way, this is also one of your largest and most valuable assets. Alexander Grant, a national CPA firm, reports that the value of every dollar in receivables declines to 80 cents after 120 days, 67 cents after six months, and 45 cents after one year.

How many days collection time do you have in your accounts receivable? In other words, what is the average amount of time it takes to collect payment from your customers? (Once you know that, you will be able to put a dollar value on every day it takes to collect.) Here is a quick way to calculate this important statistic:

Divide your total accounts receivable (AR) by your recent, average monthly sales (MS). Next, multiply that total by the time period used in the sales figure. If you used a month's sales (average or not), multiply by 30 days. If you used an annual sales figure, then multiply by 365. The net result will be the approximate number of days to collect (NDC). (AR/MS) x 30 = NDC. Try this formula on the sample:

Divide the Accounts Receivable, $100,000, by the average monthly sales of $34,500.

1. 100 divided by 34.5 = 2.9

   Multiply the result by 30 (representing days).
2. 2.9 times 30 = 87, which translates into 87 days average collection time. (100/34.5) x 30 = 87

The above example shows that it would take an average of 87 days to collect the accounts receivable (almost three months). Considering that 30 days are normal credit terms for most industries, 87 days is outrageous and very costly.

The impact of poor collections can best be illustrated by telling the story of a small oil company that went to their bank to borrow money for additional working capital. To make the loan, the bank wanted to know some significant facts about their operation, such as the number of days it takes to collect. The oil company did not keep good records, and certainly nothing in that fashion. They could not answer the bank's questions so they hired an accountant to develop this information. Along with preparing those numbers, the accountant set them up with a One-Write system that enabled the oil company to get an aging, and he also taught them how to handle the collections properly.

When the oil company originally went to the bank, they were seeking a $20,000 loan. Three months later, after the new system was installed, the documentation was prepared for the bank. But a strange thing occurred while preparing the documents. They discovered that their days required to collect were originally 66. That number had dropped from 66 to 44, a reduction of 22 days. They also realized that they did not have the money pressure they were experiencing three months prior. Analyzing the data, they found that their cash flow had improved by $24,000. Moreover, they no longer needed the $20,000 they were trying to borrow. By collecting the old accounts receivable and reducing the average collection time of the total accounts receivable, they were able to generate an additional $24,000. Look at it this way: A reduction of 22 days average collection time equaled $24,000. That equates to about $1,091 per day. What is the dollar value of every day of collection time worth to you? Do you think that you should put some effort into that area?

If you have a computer, make sure that you send monthly statements to your customers. If you do not have a computer nor want one, use a One-Write system. If your computer system will not allow you to get an aging or send statements, then scrap it and start over with another program.

According to Alexander Grant (the CPA firm), $200,000 would only be worth $160,000 at the end of 120 days, so poor collections cost $40,000 in this illustration. Your CPA can help in setting up good procedures to assure timely collection of receivables. Here are some methods for increasing cash flow through the accounts receivable:

1. Reduce accounts receivable by collecting faster.
2. Sell more on a cash basis (consider offering discounts).
3. Put slow pay accounts on COD quicker.
4. Always check credit before shipping merchandise.
5. Require partial or full payment with new orders.

Nowadays, accounts receivable financing is commonplace. An asset-based lender will advance 70% to 85% of your current receivables. You may already have this arrangement with your bank. In all cases, these lenders will only finance receivables that are 90 days and less in age. If your customers take more than 90 days to pay, they will reduce your availability by the total amount of their invoices. This policy is a double-edged sword. For example, a publishing company had this type of accounts receivable financing. They were at their limit with the bank, and there was no more availability. At the same time cash got very tight. The company did not know where to turn. Simultaneously, vendors were threatening to put them on credit hold. While this crisis was taking place, the company had more than $200,000 in unqualified accounts receivable (more than 90 days old). Some were totally uncollectable. But, as it turned out, more than $100,000 was collectable. They put the effort toward that goal, and, within two weeks, the cash crunch emergency was over.

ORDER PROCESSING

Look at cash flow beyond just accounts receivable collections. It actually begins prior to billing the customer. If you will believe this, you will understand the importance of how long it takes to process, fill, and ship that order. The faster you operate, the faster you will generate capital.

The opposite effects of the above theory can be best illustrated by a horror story about a company in the office supply industry:

Typically, when they received an order from a customer, it would contain several line items. Often the office supply company would be out of at least one of the line items (a common occurrence in the office supply industry). When this would happen, the company would ship the items they had in stock and back order the item or items that were out of stock. The out-of-stock item would be ordered from a local wholesaler or directly from the factory. Coming from a local wholesaler only took a few days. On the other hand, if they ordered the item from the factory, it could take more than 30 days.

To simplify their paper flow the company did not bill the customer until the order was shipped complete. They held the incomplete order in a suspense file while they purchased and waited for the back order. When the back order arrived, they would ship it to the customer and invoice them for the entire order.

Sounds simple enough, doesn't it? What the office supply company did not realize was the subsequent effect on cash flow. In the best scenario, at least one week was added to the number of days to collect.

Adding just one week to collect was the best scenario. What about back orders that had to come from the factory? They delayed cash collection weeks longer. In this example, the investment in goods already shipped and the labor and overhead dollars tied up waiting amounted to a tidy sum. They should have originated a separate invoice for back-ordered items. Along with that, they should have sent an immediate billing for the original invoice (for merchandise shipped).

ACCOUNTS PAYABLE AND INVENTORY

Accounts payable and inventory are always good sources for generating an increased cash flow. This is how it can be done:

Suppose sales are $100,000 per month, and your usual gross margin is 40%. Based on that, you will purchase $60,000 per month to replace the inventory used for the sales made each month. By controlling the purchases and the payments to vendors, you can, in effect, gain additional cash flow.

Start by creating a purchase worksheet and a sales worksheet. This can be done by using a spreadsheet program on a personal computer, or as an alternative, you can install a simple One-Write accounts payable system (with a vendor ledger). As purchases are made (when you receive the vendor's invoice), you record these vendor invoices on a purchase journal or on a worksheet. Simultaneously, when you bill sales, record the sale on a sales journal. The next step is to make comparisons between the journals or worksheets. You do that by subtotaling both on the same date. The totals will tell you how much you have purchased and sold at a particular point in time.

For example, suppose you decide to subtotal your worksheets on the 15th of the month, and, for illustration purposes, say that the sales journal/worksheet shows that you have sold $40,000 so far. Using the previous example, your usual estimated gross margin is 40%, which means that you used $24,000 of your inventory to support those sales.

Next, look at the subtotal of the purchase worksheet. If purchases amounted to $19,000 in the same period, $5,000 less than replacement, that $5,000 will become a gain on cash flow next month or whenever the payment for those purchases is made.

Continuously monitoring the purchase relationship compared with sales will enable you to effectively reduce inventory. If you are wondering if it is worth the effort, the answer is "yes!" The reduction of inventory levels can have a significant, positive financial impact. To examine this further, you must understand "inventory turns" and what that actually means.

Simply stated, "inventory turns" is the amount of time your inventory will last at current sales levels. In other words, how many times would you have to totally replace your inventory in order to supply the annual sales? How often does your inventory turn over in a year? If your hypothetical answer is "six turns," that means you have on hand a total inventory that will support two months of sales. Four turns would support three months of sales, and so on.

The more turns in inventory, the less capital you will require to support the sales. The reason is that your dollar investment on the shelf is minimal. Here is a demonstration:

The inventory levels of the hypothetical business used in the previous example was $650,000. If sales average $100,000 per month at a 40% margin, the replacement inventory would be $720,000 for a one-turn inventory level. The company is turning their inventory at 1.1 turns. The ideal number of turns for this hypothetical enterprise is between 3 and 4 turns. When translated into dollars, the inventory value should be between $180,000 to $240,000, instead of the $650,000 current level.

The model just built exhibits some interesting phenomena. If one turn equals $720,000 and 1.1 turns equals $650,000, there is a difference of $70,000. Then going from 1.1 to two turns lowers the inventory value to $360,000 — a reduction of $290,000. Carrying this line of reasoning further, a reduction to the industry average of four turns increases cash flow by an additional $120,000 and a grand total from the current level of $410,000.

Obviously, in the real world, major inventory reductions like those mentioned above cannot occur rapidly, nor do they have to occur rapidly. They must just happen steadily. The first step may only accomplish an achievement of one-tenth of one turn. That still equates to a $70,000 increase in annual cash flow.

There are basically two primary methods to reduce inventory. The first was covered with the purchase comparison to sales control worksheet. The second method is more difficult, because it requires some specialized knowledge — a determination of how often the items in your inventory sell. This is called an ABC analysis.

The object is to create a document showing which inventory items sell most often. This may require analyzing many invoices. The inventory items that account for 50% of your sales are called "A" items. The inventory items that account for the next 25% are called "B" items. The inventory items that account for the bottom 20% are called "C" items. The rest are considered "D" items and are not important.

The next step is to value the inventory by how many dollars you have tied up in the A, B, and C items. You should have 80% of your inventory in the A and B items. Unfortunately, if you are typical, you will have 20% of your inventory in the A and B items. Because it may be normal does not make it right. It just makes it a fact of doing business that you have to deal with. Well managed companies have installed measures to prevent this imbalance, and because of those systems, they have been able to reduce inventories to much faster turns, thereby freeing up valuable cash.

Many entrepreneurs never learn the lesson of the 80/20 rule. They claim that they cannot sell from an empty cart, and that the more inventory they have, the more potential there is for sales. No doubt there is a certain amount of validity to that concept. But, it can also be untrue, as illustrated in the following story:

A wholesale auto parts distributor insisted that his growth was attributable to the amount of inventory he carried. In the early years of his company's development, this theory held true, and his growth was tied to the amount of inventory on hand. As time went on, his sales and inventory levels grew together. Then something happened to change the trend. Sales leveled off, but inventory kept on growing. Most of the inventory growth was financed with borrowed money. The situation was, unfortunately, not dealt with on a quantitative basis. Then sales dipped. The owner had no more borrowing power and was not able to increase the inventory. So he blamed the drop in sales on the lack of sufficient inventory. His general assessment was partially accurate.

A careful examination of the financial statements proved that the inventory continued to increase even though sales were going down. Yet, it was obvious that the sales order fill rate had dropped to 75%, a dangerously low number. Accordingly, the owner continued to blame the drop in sales on lower inventory levels. Because of his finances, he was not able to buy more inventory and sales fell even more. The order fill rate dropped to 60%. When the business finally closed down, two things were brought to light. First, total inventory dollars were almost at the highest level ever. Second, most of the inventory was obsolete or, at best, only turning once a year. Some inventory items were only turning once in four years.

This scenario is not unusual. It happens, to varying degrees, in almost every organization. The smart ones recognize the problem sooner, and they deal with it. The rest keep borrowing money to support out of control inventory growth, and some even go under.

In a turnaround, this inventory imbalance can be a hidden source of additional cash. The challenge is to unlock it. In Chapter 5 you learned some of the ways to convert inventory into cash. Now you need to know how reducing inventory levels can create and increase cash.

The main tool for controlling inventory is the ABC analysis. To refine the system, set up another worksheet or computer program to determine how many weeks of supply you have on hand of each of the A, B, and C items. Calculate the time it takes to get replacement inventory, and then allow yourself to run the inventory down as close to the run-out level as possible. Always allow a small cushion for some unforeseen delay. You can even allow yourself to run out of some C items. In any respect, do not reorder any D items—ever! You may have adequate supplies on hand and have no need to be concerned about it, however, if you get an order for an out-of-stock D item, buy only what you need to fill that order, even if you pay a premium for the item. The system sounds complicated and labor intensive, but most computer inventory programs can accommodate it. Remember this: your inventory and accounts receivable may contain more dollars than any other assets. Moreover, these assets are liquid and much easier to convert to cash. So, if it seems like a lot of work, try to realize that the effort is worth the result.

ACCOUNTS PAYABLE

The next piece in the cash flow puzzle is how you handle your accounts payable. Most entrepreneurs have learned, at one time or another, which vendors will allow delayed payments. Some vendors will immediately cut you off once you fall behind on your payments. Others do not seem to care how quickly or slowly you pay, just as long as you continue to pay on a regular basis. By setting up a vendor ledger card for each of these suppliers, you can control the payments according to your money inflow, while, at the same time, staying in harmony with individual vendor's collection policies. If you are presently using a One-Write disbursement system, convert it to an accounts payable system including the vendor ledger. You will find this conversion easy, and it will automatically record the transaction to the vendor ledger without additional writing or work. Your computer system can also give you this information with some program modifications.

The vendor ledger cards will show all the purchases and payments, separated by each vendor. The cards will also show the current outstanding balance owed to an individual vendor. You can also record special notes on the card such as the date that you promised to send a check.

With this information ready, you can now begin to do some special accounts payable planning.

Many vendors require immediate or prompt payment. For those that make it critical, you must mark their cards with a red signal. Mark those vendors that will call you when they want a payment with a yellow signal. Leave the rest uncoded.

Next, create a worksheet calendar. You can use a real calendar for this purpose. Review your "red" coded cards one by one. Look at the purchase transactions and record the amount due on the date due on your worksheet. Do not pay anything you do not have to pay. If a vendor requires you to pay promptly, be sure to take the cash discount. (By the way, you are also entitled to a cash discount on COD's.) After you have gone through all the red coded cards, go through the cards with the "yellow" code. Mark on your worksheet calendar the amount and date that you promised a payment, nothing else. You do not have to pay anything you did not promise to pay.

The balance of the cards should not be dealt with until you are required to do so. For example, if you are told by a vendor that you will not get any more merchandise unless you make a payment, or if the salesman asks you about the account, then make the minimum payment necessary to get shipment and to stay on open account. This becomes a negotiation. You may even offer payments spread out over a period of time, however, under no circumstance allow yourself to be put on COD.

As you make determinations on the uncoded cards, code them red or yellow as necessary. You may find certain vendors will continue to give you credit without ever calling you. This may even go on for six months or more. Do not concern yourself. When it becomes important to them, they will call you or they may even refuse to make a shipment to you unless you pay some of the old invoices. No matter how long it seems, do nothing until they ask you to make a payment. When that happens, do whatever is necessary to remain on open credit with that vendor.

Do not become a "dead beat" who does not pay his bills. Being current with your vendors is an important philosophy. However, turnarounds are slightly different, because, without adequate funds, staying afloat can be tenuous. If there were an abundance of cash, then, some of these strategies would not be necessary.

How much additional capital can you generate by frugal manipulation of the accounts payable? Using the previous hypothetical example, take a look at the possibilities:

Sales were about $100,000 per month, and the gross margin was 40%, which means that it requires $60,000 per month to replace the inventory used to support those sales. There is probably another $10,000 per month in general (non-payroll) expenses. So, with this example in mind, the current accounts payable is about $70,000 per month. Consequently, if it were possible to delay payments on the accounts payable an additional 30 days, it would generate approximately $70,000 more cash flow. Delaying payments an additional 45 days increases cash to more than $100,000. Be cautious; not all vendors will let you go 60 days. Yet, some vendors will let you go as long as six months. However, the total average can almost always be squeezed at least 30 days.

Now, go back and add up the calendar worksheet to see how much money will be required to keep the organization going. Total this on a daily basis. Issue checks on Wednesdays, because they will normally arrive at the vendors on Fridays. This will give you the weekend as an additional float. Making disbursements once a week is usually sufficient. There will, on occasion, be times where a disbursement will have to be made outside of your schedule to appease an unhappy vendor. Do not make them wait unless you truly do not have the money to pay them. Treat your vendors as kindly as you can; they can be the key to your survival. Have your bookkeeping department give you a daily cash report which looks something like the following form:

DAILY CASH REPORT

BEGINNING CASH BALANCE________DAY____DATE_____

ACCOUNTS RECEIVABLE PAYMENTS________________

CASH SALES________________________________

CHECKS ISSUED______________________________

ENDING CASH BALANCE_________________________

MEMO

PAYROLL DUE________________AMOUNT__________

ACCOUNTS PAYABLE DUE________AMOUNT__________

FIXED EXPENSE DUE____________AMOUNT__________

FIXED EXPENSE DUE____________AMOUNT__________

FIXED EXPENSE DUE____________AMOUNT__________

With the use of the calendar worksheet, the vendor ledger cards, and the daily cash flow report, any manager can easily manage cash. Unfortunately, many managers would prefer to borrow the money from the bank rather than take the time to work the accounts payable as described here. Naturally, it will require more work; that is the down-side. The up-side is that the money you are able to borrow from your vendors is interest-free, and that can amount to a tidy sum of money.

REVIEW

1. Realize that cash is critical.
2. Banks want to know your cash position particulars.
3. Reduce the number of days to collect your accounts receivables.
4. Shorten the order processing time.
5. Increase the number of turns of your inventory.

6. Use an ABC analysis of your inventory.

7. Delay payments on accounts payable.

Usually, the first signal of a financially troubled business is poor cash flow. Cash flow by itself is not the reason that an enterprise gets into financial trouble; it is usually the result of the trouble. Sometimes the cash flow deteriorates because of serious systems neglect. That neglect causes many problems throughout the organization, and often this is what makes a turnaround necessary.

When you have cash flow problems, it is not a question of who is at fault. No matter how you analyze the situation, it is still your responsibility. Now is the time to take control and make things happen. Be pro active and not reactive.

Chapter 11

CUTTING BACK PAYROLL COSTS

Payroll is usually the largest single expense of a business, with the possible exception of the cost of goods. Certain types of professional and small mom-and-pop organizations are excluded from this aphorism. Nonetheless, payroll dollars are sizable, and often they are the number one place to cut.

Each industry has its own statistics concerning normal payroll expenses. As a guide, payroll expense may vary from about 10% of sales to over 30% of sales. Check out your own industry averages. It may be an eye-opening experience to see how you stack up against some of your competitors and fellow business people. However, these industry averages, whether you are above or below, have no meaningful value in a turnaround. No matter what your industry average may be, you will still have to cut payroll expenses. Naturally, if your company payroll is running way ahead of your industry average, you will feel better about making some cuts. On the other hand, if your payroll percentages are in line or under your industry average, you may have a difficult time convincing yourself that layoffs are in order. If you give in to those feelings, that will be your undoing. You must still cut back on the payroll expense, no matter what your current staffing numbers are or how they relate to your industry averages.

Eight fundamental elements that deal with payroll expense cutbacks are:

1. Quantity of personnel
2. Overtime pay
3. Hourly pay and salary scale levels
4. Union considerations
5. Fringe benefits

6. Work rules
7. Work hours
8. Employee attitudes

Understanding these can have a significant impact on the payroll expense. Moreover, you must have an objective in mind with each of these elements before proceeding. These objectives may seem simple and uncomplicated, and they shouldn't be too difficult to understand or implement. Before starting with an objective plan, review what options are available to you with each of the eight elements listed above.

QUANTITY OF PEOPLE

The first step in the process is to analyze your "people numbers." Your first impulse is to say that you are down to the bare bones already and there is no more room for cuts. Why would you have extra people around anyway? For the most part, this is probably true, but you may be staffed at the same level you were when sales were 15% greater than what they are today. That is why a careful analysis must be made—and made objectively, not subjectively. Try to look at your own organization as if it were someone else's company. Be as critical as you can.

Once you have completed your analysis, you may discover that you could do without a few nonessential employees. Before you let anyone go, wait until you have a complete plan of action. Of course, if anyone leaves, you do not replace them unless it is a critical position. Even then, could someone from the inside do the job on a temporary basis? If so, move them into that vacant spot. Perhaps you may not have to replace the person you moved into that spot. Maybe that person can do both jobs. In any event, personnel cuts are only a small part of the payroll picture, and a "meat ax" approach may not be necessary to trim down your staff.

Here is a trap: The typical cutbacks usually come at the lower levels, such as secretaries or shipping clerks. Very often, when these levels are cut back, critical work does not get done. Look at what work your people do. Perhaps some of this work is not essential to the survival of your company. If you cut out nonessential people, then that is a good cut. If the work is critical, then the cut is not so good.

For example: An office furniture company had some financial difficulties, so they cut back some of their people. The cutbacks were in two areas, marginal salespeople and clerical staff. The company soon discovered that these cutbacks caused two additional problems: Sales decreased a little, thereby compounding the financial problems, and the clerical cutback meant critical paperwork was not done. Orders were not placed in a timely way, invoices were not checked, billing was delayed (causing more financial problems), and a host of other important duties fell through the cracks. Sure, payroll was cut back a little, but the cost was too great.

Interestingly, there were two high-level managers doing the same work, the salesmanager and the vice president, general manager. This would have been an ideal time to evaluate the necessity of having two top executives. The cutback of either one would have saved four to five times the salary of one of the clerical people and probably not have had much adverse effect. Unfortunately, it is more common to cut back personnel at the lower levels, even though it is more effective to cut at the top.

There are no set rules to determine who to cut. Top managers and clerical staff should both be targets for contemplation. Consider this situation in a company where sales had fallen off 33%, yet not one person was let go in the shipping department. In fact, there was still a considerable amount of overtime. The department manager was very protective of his people and did not want to let anyone go. So, he made a lot of excuses. On one occasion, he said that even though business was off one third, he still had to ship the same amount of orders. It was the quantities that were lower, and, because of that, it still took all those shipping people to get out the orders.

Upon closer examination, it was discovered that work did expand to meet the time available. In other words, employees found "busy work" to do when there were no orders to fill.

Later, in management meetings, the department head defended himself by putting the blame on the sales department for not bringing in the business. He used a strong offense as his defense. Later, he admitted that he could handle a third more orders with the same staff. Even then, management still did not make any cuts in his department.

The point of the above illustration is to show how difficult it is to cut back on people. Still another company had two delivery trucks going out every day. Sales had dropped 50% from normal for three months in a row. When the manager was asked to cut back some people, he honestly did not know where to cut.

Eventually, he combined the delivery routes and eliminated one person and a truck. But it took a month before he would do it; and then it was because he was forced into doing it. Employee cutbacks do not happen unless the leader decides to make them expeditiously. A strong-willed and determined leader will communicate his desires to his management team (if he has one), because they have to be committed, too or it will not happen.

OVERTIME PAY

The second element of payroll expense reduction is overtime pay. Because of the laws of the land, you are restricted to a great extent. If a non-exempt, hourly employee works overtime, you must pay time-and-a-half. However, you are the one determining whether or not that person works overtime, so just put a stop to overtime. Once again, this is easier said than done. There are dozens of situations that will require overtime. Sometimes you will have to allow it. But, for the most part, you must stop overtime.

Overtime costs you an extra one and a half times the regular hourly pay. If the work absolutely needs to be done, try putting management on it. They are exempt from overtime laws and do not require extra pay. If they are supportive of the turnaround, they will work any amount of hours necessary to save the business.

To illustrate the cost of overtime further, look at the cost if only 20% of your work force put in one hour per day of overtime. (This is really an absolute minimum.)

Suppose you have 20 employees averaging $960 per day at regular pay. This amounts to $4,800 per week. The overtime illustration as outlined above would cost you an additional $180 per week, or $9,360 per year. What if your actual labor is double that of the illustration? That could amount to almost $20,000 a year for overtime!

SALARY REDUCTIONS

After you have discontinued most of the overtime pay, you must now deal with regular pay cuts. Lee Iacocca said that he started by reducing his own salary to one dollar per year. Then, he started in on the executives. He cut their salaries by up to 10% (Other companies have cut up to 15%). He also cut salaries up to the lowest levels, leaving the secretaries alone. He felt that they deserved every cent they made. Next came the unions. He said that in a 19-month period, the average working guy at Chrysler gave up close to $10,000.

Iacocca also said that he learned a lot about people in trying to save Chrysler. He discovered that people accept a lot of pain if everybody is going through the chute together. He called this "equality of sacrifice." It worked for Iacocca and Chrysler; it could work for you as well. Just make sure that your pay cuts are fair and equal among *all* employees, including you and your management staff.

UNIONS

Handling unions takes a little talent. Fortunately, union leadership, for the most part, is interested in saving jobs. Therefore, they will listen to you if you are genuinely having a financial problem.

Your presentation to the union is very important; therefore, you must carefully plan your strategy. The first step is to get your information together. Have all your financial records ready to show to the union leadership. Be honest with what you show them. Next, call for a meeting on your premises. Explain to them exactly what the problem is as you see it and what you are doing about it. Also let them know, in clear terms, what they can do to help save the company.

Know exactly what you are going to ask for. Show them that you are prepared to insist on management cuts also. Let them review your plan to save the company so that they can see that you are attacking the financial problems on many levels, not just on union employee wages.

Even if the union leadership is sympathetic, they will, most likely, not make a decision that day. They may bring their lawyer along to meet with you. They may even want to meet with the employees. They may not take any action at all (even after they say they will do something).

You are the key motivator and the person who can get the union off dead center. You do this by persistence. Do not let up, or you will lose. You may have to call them every day until you get what you want. More important, you must let them know how critical it is for them to get you some wage and work rules relief. Understand that it will be uncomfortable and difficult for them to approach the rank and file. Consequently, they will procrastinate. Who knows? They might believe that maybe your problem will go away or fix itself without their help. This may be true, but do not let them off the hook; keep pushing or they may not come through for you. Remember, there are two underlying threats that the union cannot ignore: the possibility of the business closing down, which means a loss of jobs, and the possibility of a Chapter 11 filing, which can terminate or set aside the union contract.

FRINGE BENEFITS

The fifth item on the list is fringe benefits. Fringe benefits are very expensive, and the average employee honestly does not know what you spend on him for his fringe benefits package. That makes fringe benefits a good place to make some cuts.

To give you some idea of what can be done, consider this story about a wholesale nursery that had 11 employees. About 70% were female and married. When things turned bad, the owner forced his employees to pay for their own medical insurance. Except for three employees, everyone else elected to drop out of the program. The net savings was about $2,000 per month.

What happened? When the company supplied free medical insurance, everyone took it. Why not? It seems that most of the employees were also covered under their spouses' insurance plan. As a result, when they were asked to pay their own insurance premiums, most of them said, "Why do I need it? I'm covered on my husband's policy."

Look at the entire fringe benefit package closely. Perhaps you may find some other cuts as well.

WORK RULES

One of the most neglected areas of the payroll commitment is work rules. This is an area where productivity and dollars can be made or wasted. Sometimes work rules and fringe benefits are interrelated, because many of the work rules are defacto fringe benefits to the employees. For example, when does overtime start in your company? Do you ever pay double time? How do you treat employees who work on Saturday? What are your shift premiums? How many employees do you assign to a particular function? What is your sick pay policy? What is your paid vacation policy?

Evaluate your entire program. That is not to say that you can eliminate everything. That is impossible to do without doing greater harm to the organization. It all depends on how critical things are. If it means that you are going broke, then perhaps you had better look at work rules more closely. There is always a place where some cuts can be made.

For example, there was a printing company whose very large printing presses required several people to run them. It was customary for some employees to do certain functions only, (nothing beneath their position) on that piece of equipment. During a company financial crisis, the key and senior employees were told of the financial problem. They came up with the idea of reducing the manning requirements, and they volunteered to take on those tasks themselves. This alone reduced plant payroll costs by 10%. Moreover, it turned out that productivity also went up, even though there were fewer people on the shift.

In another situation, a company was running three shifts when sales dipped about 15%. This was really not enough of a drop to eliminate the third shift because it would produce a short fall of needed product. Management discussed the problem with the key and senior employees, and together they figured out a way to make staff reductions on two shifts and cut half the employees on the third shift. The result was that they were able to produce almost as much as they did when they ran three full shifts. Payroll was cut back, and productivity increased at the same time.

Most companies do not work at maximum productivity, which explains why you can very often cut back on staff and still get equal production. If you do not believe it will work, think about it in reverse. How many times have you seen the same staff produce more when there are more sales than normal? What happens when you get especially busy? Doesn't the work somehow get done? Isn't it true that the busier you get, the more productive your organization becomes? Haven't you ever noticed that when your company has made a lot of money in any one month, it was because sales were way up, and you were able to produce it with the same staff size and overhead?

WORK HOURS

Another way to cut down on the payroll is to cut back work hours. Why not? When sales are down, work declines in some proportion to the slack. Therefore, it is entirely acceptable to cut back on work hours. For example, if your employees normally work a 40-hour week, there is nothing in the rule book that prevents you from cutting back to a 32-hour work week.

You can selectively reduce the hours of any employee without breaking employment laws. Be very careful how you do that, because you do not want to appear unfair. If that happens, you will lose any benefit you may have gained in payroll savings by poor employee attitudes, and in some cases, they may even sabotage your efforts.

Going to a four-day week can also work. You can give some of your people Friday off, and some of your people can take Monday off. That way you are covered five days a week. The disadvantage is that two days a week you are working with a half staff. It will take some real organization to overcome that problem.

In many areas of the country (but not all) the department of employment will pay unemployment benefits to your employees for the loss of their time due to cutbacks. It works this way: You pay them for the four days on a regular payroll basis. The department of employment pays them unemployment compensation for the one day. Between the two paychecks, the employees can come out very close to their regular earnings. That way you can cut back your payroll 20% without the risk of losing any employees. You even have the ability to bring them back to a fulltime status any time the business requires.

Each state has different requirements, so it would be wise to check personally before you make any plans. They will also tell you how it is done and how your employees file a claim. Usually, this work-share program will last six months to a year and can be very valuable to you, so don't pass it by.

Although each business turnaround is different, the one common feature is that the business needs help. If the kind of help you need involves recovering from operational losses, then you must consider payroll cuts. The severity of your problem determines how deep the cuts must be, however, you should have a goal in mind. Suppose you want an overall payroll cut of 15% (usually a good number), then you should prepare a plan of action that will achieve that goal.

EMPLOYEE ATTITUDES

Without the support of your management team and your employees, your efforts will fail. Their attitudes can make or break your attempt to cut back on payroll expenses without killing the business. Moreover, they do not want to cut their pay, consequently, you will be wise to bring in your key employees to consult on where and what you can do. Have them involved from the very beginning of the planning cycle. Solicit their help. Make everybody a part of the problem and solution. If you are fortunate, you will be able to get the power of your employees on your side. This power can, very often, be the deciding point in whether or not your turnaround is successful.

REVIEW

1. Start by evaluating all your employee staffing needs.

2. Reduce overtime, or eliminate it if possible.
3. Give pay cuts if possible.
4. If you have a union, bring them into the problem.
5. Look at cutting back on fringe benefits.
6. Try cutting back on hours.
7. Set goals.
8. Enlist the help of your employees.

Every phase of a turnaround is difficult, and payroll expense cuts are probably the most difficult of all, and yet, they are very significant because of the dollar amount involved. Most people believe that payroll cuts are the last thing that should be looked at. Because of this attitude, they very often wait too long to do anything about it. They let many excuses get in the way, and, because of that, sometimes nothing happens at all.

In essence, you should look at payroll expense as just another element in your company turnaround. Make a plan and then carry it out. Be sure to get the support of your employees or it will not work.

Chapter 12

FOURTEEN IDEAS FOR REDUCING EXPENSES

This book outlines and discusses seven predominant elements of business operations. The management of these elements has a profound significance on a successful turnaround. Now, we come to expenses. Some professionals start with this element because cutting expenses is easy. At least it appears that way until you actually get into the task of expense cutting. It never fails. It always seems that just about everything, for some reason or another, cannot be cut out.

Realistically speaking, every operation has many expenses that should be cut and sometimes eliminated. But, when you delve into the actual job of determining where to make specific cuts, you always seem to come up with a good reason why it is not practical right now to make that particular adjustment.

For example, there was a small publishing company that was in financial trouble. Because of that, they brought in a new general manager. He knew that his cost of supplies was out of line with the industry standards by about 11%. He spoke with his management team as well as those responsible for the purchasing. He told them that he expected expense reductions and that supply purchases were an easy target to cut. He felt that a 5% cutback was a worthy goal. Was he in for a real surprise! When he tried to solicit support for his 5% goal, his people looked at him as if he was crazy. They started hurling invectives at him for even suggesting they were unnecessarily overbuying. "After all," they said, "we only bought what we needed." The new GM still insisted that cuts could be made, so he set up a system to monitor and control purchases. Every intended purchase was written up on a purchase request form, and each form had to be submitted to him and explained. He also required his people to write the cost on the request form and he would only sign the form after he was satisfied that the quantity and cost were in line. Sometimes he cut back on the quantity if it was more than a 30-to-60 day supply. Occasionally, he would refuse to sign the form if there was not enough information. In other words, he made his managers manage the purchasing.

That simple system alone accounted for the following results. Over a nine-month period, purchases went down about 10% on average. Simultaneously, sales increased about 20% during the same period. The net result was that purchases of supplies came in line with the industry's standard percentages, a significant improvement over what existed before.

Nine months later, the general manager called his managers together and showed them, in black and white, the results. They looked at him with astonishment. As far as they were concerned, they did not change their behavior at all. They were doing the same thing they always did; they only bought what they needed. Even in the face of strong evidence, they still denied the real truth. Fortunately, the general manager did not give in. He got his way and would not settle for anything less than excellence. After all, isn't that what a leader is supposed to do?

Cutting expenses is always easier to do in someone else's business or department. It might make a great experiment for one manager to be responsible for coming up with the cuts for another manager. Perhaps the old cliche being "too close to the forest to see the trees" is accurate when it comes to expense cutting.

Unfortunately, most managers do not approach expense reductions in an objective way. They become irrational and very subjective. Your job as the leader is to motivate all your people to become involved with the job of saving the company. Expense cuts are a necessary element, and you'll have to cut with zeal. Otherwise, you might not succeed, or, at best, take much longer than necessary to solve the problems of the company.

There are numerous opportunities in every business where expenses can be cut. Since payroll, purchases, and supplies have already been dealt with, they have been left off the following list:

FACILITIES

Do you have more space than you absolutely need? Can you reduce the amount of space you are renting or using? If you have extra space, have you tried to rent it to someone else?

Here are two real-life stories which best illustrate how money can be saved in occupancy costs. A distribution company expanded into new facilities. Soon thereafter, they found themselves in financial trouble. They were operating out of two very large rented buildings. Each building was about equal in size, and each building was half utilized. Management went to the landlord and made a deal to get out of the lease on one of the buildings. They moved everything into the remaining facility, and, because of the consolidation, they were able to save 50% on their rent costs. Are you using more space than you truly need?

The other story is about another distribution company that rented a building and sublet half to another tenant. The sublet tenant was unable to pay the rent and vacated the premises. Strange as it may sound, the distribution company did nothing to find another tenant, nor did they contact the landlord to see if a deal could be made to get out of the lease. Even in the face of operational losses, the company still neglected to do anything about the space; they just continued to pay the rent. The company eventually went out of business. Perhaps if they had unloaded the unnecessary space, they might have survived.

UNUSUAL PERKS

Do you have any special deals that are given as fringe benefits? Is your wife getting a company credit card or car? Is your father on the payroll?

As an example, there was an engraving company that became marginally profitable. The owner's mother-in-law was a legitimate employee; only she had a special deal. She worked full-time three months of the year. For this, she received a comparable salary plus four weeks paid vacation, full contribution to the pension fund, fully-paid health and dental insurance, and a company car with its related insurances. No one ever questioned the deal because she was the boss's mother-in- law. No one ever questions these types of perquisites in good times. No one says the owner cannot be generous. It is admirable to take care of family, and no one faults that philosophy. When it became clear that the business was in a little trouble, it was time to cut out the mother-in-law's extras.

Consider every opportunity as a target for saving money, even some that seem to be minor or, at best, worth little money. In total, they do add up. A little from here and a little from there eventually make a meaningful contribution, and it is so much easier to find many small abuses than one large one.

SERVICES

Do you have an outside coffee service? Are you paying for outside cleaning services that you can handle internally? What about the gardening service? If you look carefully at every dollar spent, you can probably find a lot of services that could be eliminated or done some other way.

For example, an office furniture company had a service come in once a week to water and clean the showroom plants. To save money this job was taken over internally by the employees.

Many companies pay a coffee service to come once a week and restock the coffee supplies. As a substitute, have the employees do everything themselves, including paying for their coffee as well.

These examples illustrate how easy it is to find alternative methods that cost little or nothing at all. It only requires a will to examine every expense and a desire to eliminate redundant or marginal services.

SERVICE CONTRACTS

Service contracts are both a necessity and a luxury. It all depends on the particular service contract. Are there some contracts that you could eliminate? You can find out for sure by examining each one. Do you have contracts on things that never break down? If so, why not consider eliminating the contract?

INSURANCE

When was the last time you reviewed the cost of your health insurance program? When was the last time you got competitive bids on your workman's compensation insurance and your general liability insurance? What about life insurance? Are you overinsured? Is there cash value to that policy?

When a company gets into a little trouble, it may serve as a good excuse to examine the insurance programs. Perhaps there are cuts that can be made in limits of coverage. For example, suppose your heath insurance policy now pays 80% of the bills after a $100 deductible. You might reduce your premiums by 20% or more by changing the policy to

70% and a $200 deductible. You can save another 20% if you add a pre-authorization clause. Generally speaking, most employees will accept a slight cutback on insurance benefits, especially in a turnaround. Health insurance costs have increased so much that many larger companies are increasing the deductible limits and getting away with it. HMO's have become popular for the same reasons.

DELIVERY

Are you still putting out the same money for delivery and shipping as you were when sales were greater? If so, why?

Years ago, an aggressive catalog consumer sales company decided to try something new and innovative with shipping costs. Instead of charging the customer the actual postage or freight charges, they added handling costs to the bill. At first, they just added a fixed amount. Later, they increased the charges to include the cost of packaging, thereby adding a flexible charge based on the size of the order. Today many catalog sales companies operate this way. The customer accepts it as normal.

In another industry, (business check printing) a company shipped, via mail and UPS, about 800 packages a day. They charged the actual cost to the customer for reimbursement. They later discovered that they could easily add one dollar to every invoice under the auspices of freight and handling. By this small action they increased profits about $800 per day and produced a net gain to the bottom line of $208,000 for the year. Not one customer ever complained or even noticed the freight charges. Today, so many companies do the same thing that it has become an accepted practice.

Finally, there is a classic story about a printing company that delivered everything freight free. The customer never saw a freight charge, even if the merchandise had to be shipped clear across the country. Under the reigns of a new manager, they began a carefully planned program for charging the customer for freight costs. The freight billings during the first six months into the new program came to about $20,000 per month, a very nice addition to the bottom line. It was a "fait accompli," however, it was not easy to convince his own people that it would work. Everyone on the sales force argued that they could not charge freight because nobody in the industry did; and if they did charge, they would lose some of their customers. As it turned out, only a few customers even noticed it, and they were easily appeased when the charges were explained.

AUTOMOBILES

How many of your employees have a company car? How many members of your family have a company car? What is your expense policy for the use of personal vehicles?

A turnaround always presents a great opportunity to make changes in the company auto expense policy. Now you can finally clean up and eliminate some of those odd-ball arrangements that you cannot afford anymore.

Most organizations have either a very generous employee expense policy or they are behind the going rate. If you find that your company policy is liberal and among the generous, then you have a perfect excuse to cut back on those types of expenses.

Be creative in solving your problems, like the company that had a fixed auto expense for their salespeople. When the business got into trouble, they hired a consultant who insisted that the company change its auto expense policy. They changed to a reimbursement method tied to their individual sales production. In other words, the more the salesperson sold, the more money he would receive for auto expenses. The better and more productive salespeople came out just about the same, whereas the marginal or lesser productive salespeople received a lower amount of auto expense money. The company was able to cut a few dollars from auto expenses without losing one valuable salesperson because of the change.

UTILITIES

How recently have you gone over your utility bills? Do you waste heating and air conditioning? What about lighting? Do you leave the lights on more than necessary? Have you ever tried to cut back on utilities? If your answer is "no" to most of these questions, you have another opportunity to save some money.

Most operations completely forget about how much power the air conditioning system uses. They ignore it, or just don't think about it, but they should, because that is a place where great sums of money are usually tossed out the window.

Two easy routines can cut your power bills by as much as 20% or more. The first is to only heat or cool your facilities during working hours, not at night or weekends (if these are not working hours). The second is to adjust the thermostat higher or lower (depending on whether it is being used for heating or cooling) to save power. Five degrees will not really bother anyone, and it certainly will not affect productivity.

Having a firm policy of turning off the lights when not in use helps. Many organizations have already reduced light wattage by removing a third of the fluorescent tubes from the light fixtures. Concomitant with that, they have replaced 100-watt, incandescent bulbs with 75-watt bulbs.

In one Southern California factory, they turned off the air conditioning and heating and only turned it on when the weather was extreme. They claim that it did not adversely affect productivity.

The task of cutting back on utilities is difficult unless you can get everyone in your organization committed to it. Discuss what you want done with your key employees (the leaders, whether they are management or not). Tell them exactly what is expected of them and seek their agreement.

Caution! Everyone will think that you are being petty, and that these activities will not render much savings. They are wrong. When you add them up, they could easily equal the salary of one or perhaps two or more employees. If you give your key people a choice of cutting utilities or people, which do you think they will choose?

TELEPHONE

Everyone knows that telephone expense are too high. It is like the weather; everyone talks about it, but no one does anything about it. A pro active approach is rarely taken with telephone expenses. Ask yourself these questions: Do you allow all people access to dialing long distance, or do you shut off certain telephones from long distance access? Do you monitor and question every telephone bill? Do you know for sure that all the telephone charges are for the benefit of your business? Are some of them employees' personal calls?

The first step in the procedure is to let everyone know that you are looking at the telephone bills. If your system can accommodate it, change the availability of long distance access from any telephone. Leave only those telephones connected to long distance that are necessary. Otherwise, have all long distance calls go through your receptionist or operator.

If you do not already use one, consider a service, such as MCI or

Sprint, for long-distance calling. Most of these services can give you a separate access code for each of your employees who requires the use of long-distance calling. That way you can monitor the expenses more accurately. Moreover, you can reduce the unnecessary or non-business calls.

ENTERTAINMENT

How many business lunches do you have? Can they be cut out? How about dinner meetings? What about your management team? Do they entertain customers and employees? Can that be reduced without hurting your sales efforts?

Experts say about 50% of all so-called business lunches or dinners are not necessary at all. They believe that not very much work is accomplished at these meetings. Furthermore, the work could be better achieved at the office.

Much entertainment is primarily for the enjoyment of the owner or manager. A healthy business can afford it, and it does make a nice perk. But when the operation needs across-the-board expense cuts to survive, unnecessary entertainment must be curtailed.

Entertaining customers is another matter. Yet, truthfully, how much of that can be modified without doing any harm? Probably more than you think. Examine everything with an eager eye, determined to eliminate everything that is not genuinely essential.

TRAVEL

Have you curtailed this activity in your organization? Have you put limits on what can be spent? Are you approving only travel that is necessary?

Usually there is an opportunity to save some money with travel expenses. First-class air travel should not be allowed; and, in a turn-around, only special or economy fares should be sought. These are abundantly available; all you have to do is ask for them, or seek out only those airlines that advertise special fares. For example, for a recent trip to Texas, one airline quoted a fare that was four times greater than one of the discount fares offered by another airline. The higher-priced airline said that they also offer discount fares if you make the reservation 30 days in advance. How often do you have the luxury of 30-day planning? The less expensive airline did not have any restrictions. Such fares are available all the time.

Hotel and meal costs are another area that is usually considered discretionary spending for the business traveler. With a little thought and concern, at least 50% of those expenses can be saved as well. As the leader, you must set the example for your employees. You must also install a new travel policy that has the savings objective in mind. Once this is done, the savings will automatically come. All you have to do is make sure that everyone is following the new policy to the letter. You can accomplish this by reviewing the travel expenses on a regular basis. Anything you do not understand or do not like, you question.

PROFESSIONAL SERVICES

What about your legal and accounting fees? Have you cut back there as well? What about consultants? Have you limited your expenses there?

The best way to cut back on professional services is to communicate with your accountant, attorney, and consultant. Tell them of your desire to save some of these expenses. Ask them what they can do to help. Let them know, if they do not already know, what your financial position is. Do not make the assumption that, because they know of your condition, they will be conservative with their billing. They may not care on that level. They are running their own business, and they also require profits. As a rule, they separate your business condition from their billing rate. If they are worried about your ability to endure, they may require that you pay them up front. If that is what is going on now, then you know they are not going to volunteer to reduce their billings. However, if you discuss it with them, often they may provide you with an alternative or two on how to save on their fees. Just remember, even a bankruptcy attorney will charge a substantial fee, knowing the business is going broke. So do not be naive; they will not be generous with you. They are not going to give you their service free.

ADVERTISING AND SALES PROMOTION

Are you spending money on programs that are automatic? Is your advertising program current, or is it something you set up a long time ago? What are the promotions your company participates in?

A financial expert once told the owner of a mail order firm that he believed at least 50% of his advertising was wasted. The owner agreed wholeheartedly. He said to the financial man, "You tell me which half is wasted, and I'll cut it out." It seems that this is the story with advertising and promotions; which is waste and which is effective? In a turnaround, the waste must be culled out of the budget. You just do not have the luxury of not knowing which program makes your sales effort.

One of the ways to examine which is waste and which is not is to closely review every dollar spent. A manufacturing organization in a similar situation discovered they were automatically advertising in a certain trade association magazine. When the manager examined the facts, he found that the contract for the ad expired two years prior. Moreover, the ad had not changed in more than two years. Did he need that ad to sustain current sales levels? Not likely, considering the company moved, and the ad contained the old address and telephone number. You may ask, "How does one continue to pay for an ad that no one knows about?" It is simple; the cost was small, $110 per month. Besides that, the original contract price was predicated on a payment plan with equal monthly billings. It eventually became an automatic payment through the accounting department. It was only because of dumb luck that someone asked about it.

There are many dollars spent on advertising and promotions that do not positively affect the sales effort. For example, business card ads in local throw-away tabloids are, for most companies, a total waste of money. Year book, directory, and other types of specific advertising are also very frivolous. And, finally, certain types of advertising specialty gimmicks such as key chains with your name on them, are also very marginal.

All expenditures should have a payoff that can justify the expense. Be cynical and approach each program on its own merit. The difficult part is to identify the programs that do support sales and leave them alone. It is like surgery; you want to cut out the unhealthy parts, and, at the same time, not kill the patient.

CONTRIBUTIONS AND SUBSCRIPTIONS

How many magazines do you and your employees subscribe to? How many groups, clubs, and trade associations do you belong to? What is the total cost of these clubs or groups?

When the business can afford these things, they are well worth the money. However, when the business has troubles, these things are the easiest to cut because they clearly do not bring in sales, nor do they immediately impact the profits in a positive manner.

In a recent turnaround it was discovered that the five key executives in the company all belonged to at least three airline clubs. The cost totaled $1,125 per year. Interestingly, travel that year had been cut by more than 75%; consequently, the club privileges were hardly even used.

GETTING STARTED

Where do you begin? It does appear overwhelming when you try to decide where to cut expenses. How do you specifically go about it? To begin with, you look at your last financial statements. Go directly to the expense portion of the income statement and begin there by examining every category. Have the detail of the general ledger handy, so that you can examine each expense in detail.

The above 14 items were taken from an income statement. Your statement may be more elaborate or even less detailed. It does not make any difference; the procedure is the same. You simply look at every category, and, within each category, look at the detail of the expense. While doing that, you can make decisions right there on the spot.

REVIEW

The basic steps to cut expenses are:

1. Do not let your personnel present barriers to cutting back.
2. Look first to purchasing, then payroll, and then supplies.
3. Examine every item of expense in the general ledger.

The leader of the business must take control of the money that flows out of the organization. He must also set an example for others to follow. How can the leader ask everyone to cut back and then go out and lease a new car? As incredible as this sounds, it happens all the time. He uses the excuse that the lease was up, and says, "I had to get a new car anyway." Or he says, "My cost didn't go up. It's the same payment." Irrespective of the truth, the employees and suppliers will not support cutbacks if the leader does not set the pace himself.

Chapter 13

HOW TO INCREASE SALES

There are two common misconceptions about turnarounds. Each misconception, if believed and acted upon, can produce disastrous results. The first is the belief that all of the company's ills can be solved by just increasing sales. It is often believed that once the sales level is brought up to a so-called break-even point, the company will turn around. The other misconception is believing that sales are beyond anyone's control; therefore, they should not be dealt with at all. Moreover, some believe that intentional sales cuts are more desirable than increases. This is not true and will be explained later in this chapter.

The first hypothesis is wrong because sales, by itself, is not the answer. Yes, of course, an increase in sales may appear to give the bottom line a small infusion of hope, but, invariably, costs and expenses (in a turnaround) seem to follow the sales increases.

For example, suppose you pay $10 for an item and sell that same item for $10. You are losing money because there is no profit to cover the expenses of running the business. To continue, assume that you sell 10 a day. Increasing sales to 15 a day will show more volume; however, the losses will be even greater because there still is no profit to cover the expenses and overhead. At higher-level sales, expenses will increase; therefore, there is a potential for greater loss. That is why some experts cut back on sales, especially unprofitable sales.

Sales are the life blood of any organization. Without sales, eventually there will be no income stream. Without income, the business cannot survive—no matter how efficiently it is run. This is why misconception number two is so wrong.

Actually, a turnaround requires a balance between aggressive sales efforts and an aggressive reduction of overhead and expenses. Both in harmony, is indeed the answer. Of course, unprofitable sales should be eliminated where desirable. As a matter of fact, that is the first thing that should be examined. But, before proceeding with that elimination, you should know that there are many ways to handle unprofitable sales.

SALESPEOPLE

Once all of the other elements have been dealt with as well as possible and your organization is trimmed down to a point where it is lean and mean, all that remains is to fix and increase sales. Notice the word "fix" is used to make you aware of existing sales problems before you attack the challenge of bringing in new sales.

How do you sell your product or service? Do you have salespeople? If so, improper sales management can be very costly and grossly inefficient. There are organizations that outsell other similar organizations with the same size salesforce. Why is that? Because the other salesforce is better managed than their less accomplished counterparts. The main reason that they are better managed is that management pays attention to that area of the business.

Some owners or managers truly do not like dealing with the sales force. They would rather let the darn thing manage itself. Without qualification, it is almost impossible to expect a sales force to manage itself, or be managed minimally. For the most part, profitability goes down; maximizing resources disappears; product mix and effectiveness becomes uncontrollable. Moreover, sales increases are difficult to achieve if not unattainable.

The point of this short discourse is this: a well-managed salesforce can increase sales without a great deal of effort or resources. A well-managed salesforce can also increase or maximize profits. The choice is yours; you can throw more money at the problem, lower prices, or hire more salespeople. The other option is to closely manage the existing salesforce.

Here are some key points and questions to be aware of:

1. Examine pricing if your salespeople have that discretion.
2. Determine efforts. Are your salespeople spending too much time with unproductive accounts or the less profitable products?
3. Have you examined the commission and incentive program? Does it encourage company objectives?
4. Can you account for your salespeople's time?

5. Why are some of your salespeople more productive than others?

The biggest mistake any company can ever make is to allow its salespeople uncontrollable pricing discretion. Uncontrollable because salespeople very often say they require a certain amount of pricing discretion to remain competitive. If your industry requires pricing discretion make sure you are personally in the loop. Do not allow your salespeople to set prices as they wish without some management involvement.

To illustrate how this can get out of control, consider the story of a commercial stationery company that allowed its salespeople to set the prices to their own customers:

The company had set up a schedule of automatic pricing levels and coded the accounts so that the inside customer service people could price the invoices. However, it was the salespeople who determined the discount code. They could set discount levels as they wished and even code them to allow themselves to price the invoices.

One year, during the physical inventory, the company discovered they did not have the inventory dollars it was supposed to have. Later it was learned that the company had operated at a lower gross margin than in the previous year. Buying habits had not changed, so pricing practices were investigated. It turned out that products were being sold at lower prices than before. In essence, the salesforce was charging less to their customers, and because there were no controls in place they were the only ones who knew about it.

When the company tried to repair the damage, it discovered that the salesforce had virtual no criteria for establishing discount codes for their customers and that 80% of their customers were receiving discounts that were out-of-line with their volume. The salespeople argued that they had to give large discounts otherwise the customers would not consider changing from their present supplier. The salespeople would not entertain anything to the contrary. They had made up their minds and they had to be aggressive with the pricing.

Upon a close analysis of these accounts, the company discovered that the discounts did not increase sales volume. In fact, those customers bought at a minimum level, requiring no discount at all, let alone the type of discounts they were receiving.

To combat this, the company put into effect a detailed policy on how discount codes were to be established, but six months later, they noticed there was still no improvement in the gross margins. What happened?

When management changed the policy on automatic discounting, the salespeople (who were not managed) changed the codes to allow them to price their own invoices. In the appropriate box, they checked off the discount that they were giving the customer. The discount that they checked off was a lie. They were, in fact, giving the same prices to those low volume accounts. Only now they were telling the company that they were giving lesser discounts (by the virtue of the code box that they checked).

By now a great deal of damage had been done. Customers had become accustomed to those low prices, and the salespeople were left alone so long that they were hostile to any pricing changes. The solution that the company chose was to hire a salesmanager. Unfortunately, by then it was too late to fix things without losing a few customers and a few salespeople too.

A better solution would have been to make changes slowly and to monitor the salespeople more closely. Management should have had someone check the invoices the salespeople priced and required them to justify any discount to a customer. That way, they would have discovered what the salespeople were doing and immediately stopped it.

If management had planned the solution, they would have lost only minimally profitable customers and only those salespeople who were never going to conform to proper pricing attitudes. Interestingly, when those salespeople left the company to work for someone else, they were forced to adopt the same pricing policy they refused to accept at their former organization.

If sales management is not your strong suit, then perhaps you should give that responsibility to someone else in your company. But do not make your best salesperson your salesmanager. It takes a different type of person to be a salesmanager than it does to be a salesperson. For example, these are the qualities that each must have to be successful:

SALESPERSON	SALESMANAGER
1. Have empathy	Be dominating
2. Be persistent	Be demanding
3. Be persuasive	Be a good teacher
4. Have a strong ego/drive	Inspire confidence
5. Have product knowledge	Have product knowledge
6. Work hard	Be a good organizer of others

SALESPERSON	SALESMANAGER
7. Be customer oriented	Be an idea person
8. Have selling skills	Have a fundamental knowledge of sales technique and theory

Also, a salesmanager must be a company person who has profit-oriented qualities that are not essential to the success of a salesperson. That is why the best salesperson does not always make the best salesmanager. That is not to say that a certain salesperson could not be a good salesmanager. It is just that when management promotes a salesperson to salesmanager, they usually promote the salesperson with the highest sales volume or the salesperson with the greatest longevity. Both criteria are wrong. But they do it that way because they believe they have to do it that way. They believe that salespeople expect that. They are wrong, because most people that have been promoted (in error) to salesmanager truly did not want that job in the first place. They took the job because they felt they had to, because that was what everyone expected of them.

ANALYSIS OF CUSTOMERS

Whether you have a salesmanager or not, you must determine if your salespeople are productive. Are they calling on low volume accounts too often? To find out, you must do an ABC analysis on your customers. Begin this project by determining how much each customer buys from you (those figures are available from accounts receivable records.) Then rank them by how much they purchased. After that, you can classify them as A,B, or C customers. Show your salespeople these results, and solicit their response. Show them that their efforts would be better utilized getting new accounts or spending more time with "A" customers or potential "A" customers. Perhaps the "B" and "C" customers can be handled by telephone or a telemarketing program. As an idea, consider giving the "B" and "C" accounts to a new salesperson as a foundation to get him started. The objective here is to have your seasoned producers spend 80% of their efforts on the customers that give them 80% of their business, and only 20% of their time on the customers that give them only 20% of their business, and not the other way around.

The next thing you want to examine is whether your people are selling the wrong product mix. For example, suppose they sell mostly the items that you do not have in stock, or that you do not make a good profit on. Obviously, if you know that is specifically the case, then you can address yourself to that problem. But you do not bother with it because, most likely, you do not have any real way, on a day-to-day basis, of knowing that this is the case. If your organization is like most, then probably a lot of this sort of thing exists, only you do not know about it.

The only way to do something about this very common problem is to take the time to find out what products are sold. No matter what system you use to accomplish this investigation, you will have to look at a lot of invoices. Perhaps you can set up a worksheet and let one of your clerical people post the invoices to the worksheet by each salesperson. Once you are able to determine what is happening with your product mix, then you can install a program to rectify the imbalance, if one exists.

As with all problems, you will need to carefully communicate the solution to the people involved and solicit their support; otherwise, they will give you a considerable amount of lip service and nothing more.

COMMISSION AND REWARDS

A sales organization is driven by commission and incentives, but the wrong type of program fosters low productivity. After all, why should a salesperson excel? If you say,"For the money!" you are partly right. However, if your commission program does not reward superior performance in direct proportion to the achievement, then you can be accused of saying one thing and doing another. For example, if you pay a flat 10% commission, then the more they sell, the more they earn, right? Have you ever considered special bonuses at higher levels of sales production? These types of incentives work quite well. They encourage salespeople to reach for the higher goals. Aside from the normal commission, they will stretch for the extra reward.

The other half of the picture is non-money incentives. The best and most productive sales organizations constantly have reward programs such as achievement clubs or plaques. Many use contests with trips or premiums as the rewards.

A turnaround is a good time to make changes, and there is no better opportunity to restructure the commission and incentive program. If ever there is a time when salespeople will accept something new, it is during a total company reorganization. Therefore, if your program needs to be changed or enhanced, now is the time to do it.

SALES CALL REPORTS

There are two schools of thought on whether salespeople should fill out call reports or not. The "believers" say that it forces salespeople to work by having to account for their time. Other "believers" say that call reports help them manage the sales force.

The "nonbelievers" say that call reports are a waste of time. They say that salespeople who do not work hard will just lie about the calls anyway. They say that management does not have time to read them anyway.

Which side is right? Well, both are right, and both are wrong to some extent. With proper sales management, call reports are a good tool for the salesmanager to monitor the activities of the sales people. Yes, it is a lot of work to read them. Yet, if you use them as a sales management tool, how can that be done without reading them? Besides, it won't take long before they figure out that you are not reading them.

For example, if they suspect that you are not looking at their call reports, they will test you by putting notes on the reports. They may even ask questions by writing them on the report itself. When you do not respond, they will know that you are not paying attention to them. They may still fill out reports, but they will be inaccurate or fictitious.

One salesmanager did not have time to look at the reports, so he gave them to his secretary to read. Only she did not know what she was looking for. Occasionally, she would notice something and bring it to the attention of the salesmanager. Otherwise, there was nothing gained, and all he did was waste her time as well as the salesperson's.

MBO FOR SALESPEOPLE

Those that believe that sales people will work harder if they have to account for their time are correct to some extent. The question is, are call reports going to make them work harder? Is there some other vehicle you can use to get them to account for their time? Many believe that an MBO (Management By Objectives) program for salespeople can genuinely work. Here is how it operates:

The salesperson and the salesmanager jointly develop a set of goals or objectives. Those goals can be in the form of sales, calls, or demonstrations. Then the goals are documented and agreed upon by both parties, a contract so to speak. With an MBO program, the call reports become status reports on the objectives. Many believe that this nature of accountability works much better than standard call reports.

SALESFORCE TURNOVER

In every sales organization there are many levels of success. You will find top producers, failures, and everything in between. This is a fact of sales management life. What are you supposed to do about it? Most companies do nothing; they accept it as a part of doing business. Seasoned salesmanagers know it is a numbers game. The more people you have, the more chances you have of finding the superstars. They are constantly looking for new talent. They get rid of the failures and support the potentially successful people. There is always movement; a salesforce never stays static. That is not to say that they encourage high turnover. On the other hand, they do not keep obvious nonproducers. They get rid of them to make way for new people. Who knows? The next new person they hire may be a top producer.

MARKETING STRATEGY

There are many varieties of marketing strategies. You may even be using one or more of these methods, but then again, you might find some interesting new ideas. The following are the six types of marketing strategy:

1. Hiring outside sales people
2. Networking
3. Advertising (media)
4. Direct response
5. Telemarketing
6. Direct/indirect selling

HIRING OUTSIDE SALESPEOPLE

In order to gain immediate sales increases, you would have to hire people who already have customer followings. This is the quickest way to increase sales. There are, however, some side effects to this prescription. Hiring an outside salesperson will cause your organization to change somewhat, especially if you do not have outside salespeople now. The new person may require things that you may not be prepared to provide, such as stocking special products to satisfy his customers.

Another way to add outside sales, without the pain and problems of hiring an experienced person from competition, is to take one of your existing customer service people and move them to outside sales. The advantages are numerous. To begin with, they usually know how your company operates, and they may even know some of the customers you assign to them. Sometimes these inside people have substantial product knowledge as well. At first, they can do both inside and outside sales, depending upon your individual status. It could be a sort of slow evolution from inside to outside. The only real concern is how are you going to replace what they do on the inside? Even that may fit in with your plans for an overall reduction of staff.

Another concern might be their lack of sales experience. Because of this, there is a chance they might fail as an outside salesperson. So be aware of the risks. You may want to train the person yourself.

NETWORKING

Have you ever asked a business owner where he gets his customers? He answers by saying, "Word of mouth!" Have you ever wondered how professional people such as doctors, accountants, and lawyers get clients? The technique they use is called " networking." Networking is a method for getting new business through your personal contact and involvement in activities and groups.

For example, there was a young woman in the accounting systems business who spent much of her time getting to know the accountants in her local marketing area. The accountants had the potential of referring her service to their clients. It was possible for a typical accountant to give her as many as 50 leads a year. Leads from an accountant for an accounting or bookkeeping system were a sure thing; and, with those leads, she had a sales closure rate of about 90%.

She started by calling on them personally. Then, she invited them to lunch, each time letting them know what she was capable of doing for their clients. She attended their trade shows and tax conferences. Wherever accountants were, she was there also. In a couple of years, she built a very congenial relationship with many of the local accounting firms, and the people who worked there. This relationship paid off well. She was able to increase sales every year at astounding rates.

Another woman who was trying to get her business off the ground joined the local Chamber of Commerce. She also joined a special leads networking club. Other business people join clubs such as the Rotary Club or Kiwanis. All these are considered networking—getting business through third party help or referrals.

A young eye surgeon opened his new practice without a single patient. He started by visiting the optometrists in his area. He got very friendly with them, and when their patients needed surgery, they would refer them to the young eye surgeon. In less than one year, he had built up a very good surgical practice. He still keeps in touch with his referral sources and makes it a habit to have lunch with them on a regular basis. He considers these people his friends.

Another individual who was fired from his job after 12 years found it very easy to go into the consulting business because of the networking he had done over the years with his company's customers. He had become close to them, and he was respected as well. When they learned of his dismissal, they called and asked him to consult on special projects. The networking paid off.

Everyone in your company can be a networker; encourage all people in your company to network. It is a great way to do business.

ADVERTISING

Many companies swear by advertising, and just as many say it has little value. The key to advertising success is correct advertising. Could you imagine a laundry detergent manufacturer trying to sell their products to supermarkets without heavy TV advertising? No, of course not. The supermarket will not give a product shelf space unless there is a presold demand.

Cost prohibits most small companies from hiring an advertising agency and spending megabucks on a media campaign. But there is still potential for advertising. Many companies have done very well by using local, independent television stations for their advertising. Can you imagine the first time a car dealer went on television? Their traditional advertising medium is newsprint, yet those who have gone on television have been extremely successful. Recently, lawyers have gone on television to increase business. They say it really works.

Newsprint has always been a popular method for advertising. It has kept its popularity because it can produce results. It would amaze you to find out how many former nonmedia-using companies now recognize newsprint as an effective way to increase sales. For example, 10 years ago you would be hard pressed to find an ad in the newspaper for dental or medical services. Now it is as common as any other business ad.

Local radio is one of your best advertising bargains today. It also can produce desired results, and it is not too expensive, considering how many people you can reach with your story. Next time you hear a radio commercial that seems to be airing frequently, give the owner of that company a call and ask him how he feels about radio advertising. You will probably be impressed with his answer.

Companies with smaller budgets have hired consultants to help them design programs that fit their needs and budget. These consultants can even design public relations projects that can deliver a great deal of media exposure without much expense.

DIRECT RESPONSE

This is commonly known as other things such as direct mail, mail-out solicitation, flyer advertising, and catalog selling. Each one of these is a unique marketing device, but they all fall under the category of direct response selling.

Certain types of direct response selling are only for the "big boys," because of the tremendous cost involved. That sort of selling is a numbers game and is usually limited to high margin products. However, there is nothing to prevent you from sending out mailers describing special sales or promotions to your existing customers. For that matter, you can send out mailers or flyers to potential or prospective customers as well. It is a very effective method for getting more sales, although often a little overdone on the consumer level. The key is quantity. Sending out a 100 mailers or flyers will render very little. Sending out 10,000 will get some results. Yes it is true that your mailbox is full of advertisements, many of which you throw away. Yet, on the other hand, can you imagine K-Mart not advertising that way anymore? They do it because it still works for them.

Catalog selling is also very effective for certain types of industries. Companies that have many products usually do well with catalog sales. The basic idea behind selling your products through the catalog method involves two major tasks. First, you must develop a customer data base. This is usually a comprehensive list of customers. Next, you must prepare and publish a catalog. Very often your suppliers may already have such a catalog that can be imprinted with your company name. If you can use something like that, it can save you a tremendous amount of money and time.

Once you have a catalog and a mailing list, you can proceed to distribute the catalogs. The actual method you use depends on several components. However, the best way is to copy a good idea from someone else who is doing what you want to do. Your model does not even have to be in the same industry as you. You can copy the idea just as long as you feel that it fits for you (with some modifications perhaps). Catalog advertising can increase sales as an independent effort or just as a supplement to your existing sales efforts.

TELEMARKETING

Telephone sales used to be associated with the quick-hit marketers that had elaborate boiler-room operations — the kind of people that were here today and gone tomorrow. Fortunately, that has changed for the better. Sure, there are still many boiler-room operations around, but more and more legitimate businesses are turning to the telephone to help increase sales, and, at the same time, cut the expense of a face-to-face sales call. Done properly, telemarketing can reap abundant benefits.

It should be noted here that telemarketing covers a wide range of sales techniques. It can be used to develop leads; or it can be used to handle repeat sales; and it can be used to sell obsolete items. It can be used locally or to sell outside your immediate marketing area. It can be used for special sales or promotions. Just about anything that fits your business can be adapted to some sort of telephone campaign. Here are some examples:

An auto dealer was overstocked with year-end models, and the new-model-year autos were about to arrive. He had a problem. He gathered the entire sales force and instructed them to set up a telephone campaign. Each salesperson was required to make 50 calls per day and was authorized to make deals. By the end of the week, the dealer had sold 50% of his unwanted inventory.

In another example, a wholesale tape distributor concerned about a slump in sales made a deal with his supplier for a special tape promotion. He then put two of his best order desk people on the telephones. They called every customer they had (more than 1000). The results were significant; they increased sales that month by 25%.

A business forms sales company used the telephone for repeat business. They set up a card for every new customer and noted the approximate amount of time it would take for the supply to be depleted. About six weeks before the run-out date, the company called the customer and solicited another order. Eventually the system was set up on a computer, and every day, a new list of telephone calls was printed and distributed to the telephone people. There were two major gains the company achieved with this telemarketing program. The first was cost.

At a fraction of the expense, the telemarketing program eliminated the need of having salespeople make face-to-face calls for repeat business. The salespeople were then free to seek new business, thereby increasing their overall sales. The second benefit was the reduction of lost repeat sales to competition. Because the company was on top of the repeat order, the customer did not have an opportunity to search for a supplier; the supplier came to them instead (via telephone). Moreover, it was timed approximately when the customer needed to reorder.

Another company used the telephone to create leads. Traditionally, their salespeople solicited new business by making cold calls. Typically, they would have to make at least 25 calls before getting an appointment. After that, it would take at least three appointments to make a sale. Because of the system, each salesperson could only make about seven sales a month. Using a telemarketing program to solicit leads, it took a person 40 telephone calls to get an appointment. They also found that a telephone solicitor could make about 20 calls per hour. By relieving the salespeople of the onerous duty of cold calls, they were able to make about 28 sales per month. Of course, the salesperson paid the expense of the telephone solicitor, but look at the comparison results. The salesperson was able to pay the solicitor because his income increased 400%; so did the company's sales.

There are probably thousands of examples of how telemarketing programs can help increase sales. Even the telephone company will help you discover them. Just give them a call, and ask them about telemarketing (most offer education and training).

DIRECT/INDIRECT SALES

This category takes in a wide range of activities, many of which will be briefly touched upon now. First determine if there are other tiers of distribution available to your organization. How do you distribute your service or products? Do you sell directly to the consumer, or do you sell through a dealer or distributor? If you sell direct, consider also selling through dealers or distributors. Sometimes the two cannot work together, but there are special circumstances that do allow both tiers of distribution.

For example, there was a business forms manufacturer who was having financial problems. Their equipment was underutilized. Because of that, they had plenty of production time available for additional sales. Their main thrust was a direct sales force of about 20 people. The company had a very long history as a direct seller. But the manager needed more sales, so he hired an individual to head up a new company that operated out of the same facility. The new company sold only through dealers and business forms brokers, or distributors as they call themselves. This new endeavor got very little of the company's resources; it primarily operated as a two-person operation—the new manager and an assistant/clerk. The new manager came from that type of selling in the same industry; therefore, he had many contacts. He communicated to them through mail-outs and personal calls. In a short period of time, business started coming in, though not a great deal of it at first. The dealers were skeptical of this new company because they knew that the parent organization had a direct sales force. They did not want the parent company for competition. They were afraid the new company would let the parent company's sales force know who their customers were. When it was proven they did not operate that way, they started to get more and more business.

The dealers that were out of the area were not concerned about the direct sales force; they were only concerned about price and service. (That is the way it is in the forms industry.) Each month, dealer sales got better and better, and, after a year, dealer sales were substantial and still growing.

The direct sales force was also skeptical of this new operation. They did not want the competition either. They had to be convinced that dealer sales were not additional competition; they were already in competition (doing business with another manufacturer).

It took a bold step to get the program started. Many said it could not fit. They were wrong. The program worked because it was a win/win situation for everyone. It also worked because management did not try to pull the wool over their sales people's eyes. They communicated the problem and the solution thoroughly until they had agreement from the people who were involved or affected.

In another story, there was a business check manufacturer who had a very loyal and defined base of distributor customers. Each distributor had a specific geographic territory where he was responsible for marketing the company's products. During a very bad year, the company was not able to motivate these distributors to sell more of their products. In fact, many of the distributors started to sell other companies' products in order to pick up the slack in sales. This, of course, only exacerbated the problem for the original company.

The company made a contract with a large, national organization to do some subcontract manufacturing. The other company was, to some extent, a sort of competitor. Moreover, they did not abide by the company's geographic guidelines. Because of these circumstances, the company's distributors were against the arrangement. Eventually, the program worked, and sales increased substantially. The additional sales saved the year for the company. What was doomed to be the worst year in the company's history turned out all right.

On the surface, it appeared that, because of the way the company marketed its products, it was impossible to add another distribution tier. Certainly, if you had asked the management and the distributors, they would have told you, "No way!" Fortunately for the company, they had a very astute marketing manager who understood the problem and the solution better than anyone in the organization. He knew it could work and be a win/win situation for everyone. All he had to do was convince everyone in management and all the distributors that it was necessary for the success of the company. In the face of great odds, he proceeded, putting his job on the line, because he knew he was right and that it could work. Here is how he did it:

He started by communicating with the key distributors, the ones that would be most likely affected. Simultaneously, he communicated the problem to the potential contract customer. He and the customer became very close. As a result of that friendship, the customer helped the marketing manager over some problematic humps by making some concessions on distribution policy.

He set up a network of his key distributors to also sell some products to the subcontract customer. They became a part of his sales team. The distributors participated because they would benefit directly by increasing their own sales, something they needed as badly as the company. When the word got out that the company was working on a big subcontract deal, other distributors wanted in. There was not enough volume for every distributor, but how could anyone complain about the program since they wanted it also (even though they did not get it)? By the time the subcontract customer was ready to place orders, most of the distributors were supportive to one degree or another. Those who were against the program were unequivocally in the minority, and because they were in the minority they did not present much opposition. Since then, the company has attracted other subcontract customers. To the surprise of most, the only real growth they have had in the last few years is due to this new tier of distribution.

In yet another story, a wholesale jobber needed more sales. He was getting the most he could reasonably get from his retailers, and that was still not enough to support his overhead, so he opened several retail outlets himself. They were, of course, under a different name; however, his retailers found out about it and complained. He let them know that it was just another investment, and that he treated his own stores with the same policy that he treated his retailers. He told them that each store had to stand on its own, and that they would not be supported by the jobber. He did lose a few customers, but, for the most part, his customers stayed with him.

Even giant IBM made a change in their marketing program to some degree by opening up dealerships to sell their personal computers. Until that time, IBM was primarily a direct sales organization; they still are.

A small metal fabrication company was experiencing some sales problems. The president felt that his existing product line was at a saturation level, and he didn't believe he could get the growth from within his own company's present marketing and sales strategy. He did, however, have a valuable network of dealers that were selling his existing product line. To solve his problem, the president made a deal with a Canadian company to warehouse and distribute their products to his dealer network. He inherited the Canadian's customers as well because he made an exclusive U.S.A. distribution arrangement. This increased sales about 20% in just a few short years.

A computer furniture manufacturer who had suffered a substantial dip in sales two years in a row made a deal with a catalog distributor to manufacture an exclusive line of computer printer stands. Soon, volume was about 500 stands per week. This program doubled the company's sales.

The point of this whole discussion is this: do not box yourself in. Do not make the assumption that there is no other way to increase sales. Be creative and, more importantly, be flexible. Expand your thinking. Ask yourself, what would I do if I did not have any restrictions? Once you answer that question, then do it, irrespective of the restrictions. Create a way to solve the problems of those restrictions. Others have done it; so can you.

One last example. A small check printing company was competing against the big national firms and was losing the battle. The national check printing manufacturers dominated the banking industry, the arena where checks are sold. The small check printing firm faced eventual extinction if they continued to put all their eggs in one basket. They wanted to do something, but they were boxed in by the banking industry and the traditional method of sales. They solved the problem by going direct to the consumer. They placed ads in the newspaper soliciting orders at a discount price, and the business flowed in, except that it now came directly from the consumer and not the bank. The price they gave to the consumer was higher than what they charged the bank; however, the consumer paid less for the product because the bank profit was eliminated. The company benefited because they had no competition in this market, and they also sold at higher prices, thereby making more profit. Moreover, their existence was not tenuous anymore. They found a niche for themselves and survived.

Aside from the traditional marketing methods discussed in this chapter, there is another way to increase sales. This increase will take less effort than some of the others; however, it will take some serious thought and planning. It also requires a great deal of communication and support from the people in your own sales organization. The sales increase comes about from price increases.

Almost every business can handle a small price increase without hurting sales. Irrespective of competition, customer pressure, and a host of other reasons, price increases are easy. It is how you do it that counts.

In order to show you how, there is a story of a printing company that was in serious financial trouble. The company's specialty was publication printing. This class of business is very price-sensitive and service-oriented, and customer behavior is unique. The customers make many changes at the eleventh hour yet still expect delivery on the original schedule. This causes a great deal of overtime labor for the company. The shop was a union shop, which paid compulsory time-and-a half over seven hours and double-time on Saturday and Sunday. Ironically, the customer only paid minimum charges for the changes. Regardless of the changes, the customer expected a rigid delivery schedule, even if it required overtime, including weekends. To make things more difficult, the company had allowed this routine to go on for years; therefore, the customers veritably expected this kind of service.

When a new general manager came on board, he immediately examined the cost versus the sales and found that the prices did not take into consideration the additional costs caused by customers. Whether the company made money or not seemed to be no one's concern. The customers were not going to complain; they were getting a good deal. Many of these customers had been dealing with the company more than

10 years, and some as long as 20 years.

The first thing the new manager examined was the charge policy for customer changes. (They called this "customer alterations.") He discovered that they had a pricing policy which made any alteration which cost $50 or less not billable to the customer. Alterations that cost more than $50 were billed at cost plus 10%.

More than half of the customer alterations cost between $30 and $50. These added up to about $5,000 per month. The other half amounted to about $30,000 per month in cost and generated only $3,000 per month in profits. The overtime cost usually amounted to about $10,000 per month and up to $20,000 in the busy months. These charges were, for the most part, absorbed by the company.

The new manager gathered his management team and explained to them the objectives of the turnaround and the need to raise pricing, especially in the customer alteration area. Naturally, the majority of his team objected, especially the sales people. Eventually, the new manager won out, and a new policy was installed. Here is what he did:

He started with the charges on customer alterations. He established a minimum change order billing of $50. No matter how little the actual cost, he still insisted on a $50 minimum, even if the cost was only $20. On alterations where the cost was more than $40, there was a minimum markup of 25%, as opposed to 10%. There were certain circumstances where the alteration was worth more money, irrespective of the cost. Because of that, the new manager doubled the cost in his billing to the customer. It all depended on the value and how large the dollars involved were. To make these charges palatable to the sales people, he changed the policy to make the alterations commissionable.

The next item he addressed was the company's overtime posture. He did this by letting each customer know his individual delivery schedule and how that was related to the efforts of both the company and the customer. Every time the customer made a change or alteration, the customer was notified of the new delivery schedule. Naturally, these new schedules did not authorize overtime to meet a customer's original deadline. If the delivery schedule was amended due to the customer's making changes, and if a customer could not live with the new schedule, he was given the opportunity to authorize overtime to get the job done. Under the new policy, overtime was always billed out at a premium profit.

Finally, there were occasions when a customer needed super

delivery service (usually one or two days, though normal schedules were two weeks). When this had happened in the past, the company would only bill out a slight up-charge. Under the new policy, the customer could pay as much as 100% price premium for this extraordinary service.

How did all this affect sales? Surprisingly, it increased the sales by about $40,000 monthly, and the real prize was that it was all clear profit.

The story is not finished. The new manager felt that the normal pricing was also low. His sales organization once again disagreed. Slowly, he started to increase prices. His goal was to increase about 10%. He knew this would be difficult, and because of that, he was resolved that it would take some time to accomplish. It took a little over a year, but the results were well worth it. How did it affect the customers? Not one customer was lost owing to the new pricing.

Later, it was learned that the company was still very competitive in the market place. Can you imagine how competitive they were before the change? For some reason, the entire organization wore blinders and would not recognize the truth. Everybody blamed the salespeople. They said that the salespeople had everyone convinced that the company would lose the customers if they increased prices. They were wrong. They were just behaving like normal salespeople behave concerning price.

REVIEW

The steps and procedures involved in increasing sales in a turn-around are:

1. Carefully redefine how the company makes sales.
2. Examine the sales management procedures.
3. Look for new opportunities in the six marketing methods.
4. Redefine the pricing policy of the company for increases.

There are no panaceas when it comes to sales. There is no luck either. Sales must be carefully thought out, and a series of plans must be developed. Just as important, carry out those plans with a zeal; otherwise, nothing of any substance or longevity will happen.

PART FOUR

MAINTAINING THE TURNAROUND

Chapter 14

GETTING PROPER INFORMATION

Managing a turnaround is like hanging wallpaper. You start by carefully cutting the paper to the right size. Then you put glue on the back of the paper, carefully aligning the paper on the wall and slowly smoothing it out. You go over it again, making sure that it is on straight and that all the air bubbles have been squeezed out. Now you are ready to hang the second strip of paper.

Once again, you carefully align the second strip of wallpaper next to the first strip you hung. You make sure that it is on the wall straight, and then you take both your hands and a brush and smooth it out.

You look at your work with pride. You have successfully hung two strips of wallpaper, and they look pretty good. Carefully repeating the steps that worked before, you hang the third strip. You align the edges both at the top and on the left side. As soon as you are sure that it is straight, you begin to smooth it down.

Unfortunately, when you get about half way down the third strip, you notice out of the corner of your left eye, that the first strip is starting to peel back from the top. You stop what you are doing on the third strip, move your ladder to the first strip, and you begin rehanging it so that it will stay up this time.

While you are repairing the first strip, you notice, out of the corner of your right eye, that the third strip is starting to peel back. You just did not have enough time to get it on correctly before you had to repair the first strip. So, you move the ladder slightly to the right, and with your left hand, you hold strip number one in place while, with your right hand, you rehang the third strip. While your left hand is holding the first strip in place and your right hand is holding the third, you watch helplessly, as the second strip of wallpaper peels down on your face.

This illustrates the frustrations involved in doing a turnaround. Your careful cutting and aligning of the paper is analogous to the strategy and planning. The hanging is analogous to the implementation, and the smoothing is the same as making sure the strategy works as planned. The rest is what typically happens. The things you put in place, the things you fix, and the new procedures you install all seem to fall apart or get discarded the minute you turn your back or move on to another project.

Just as in the story, you are constantly forced to stop whatever you are doing and refix old problems and systems once again. It seems that you fix and refix the same problems again and again. Finally, you end up reacting to these problems as they happen, thereby preventing you from moving on. When that happens, you find yourself working very hard just to maintain, and the rest of your much needed plans never get carried out properly. In the end, are you any better off? Well, maybe, but certainly not to the extent that you should be. A positive note! Eventually, the wall paper sticks, and so does your turnaround. It happens by persistence, and, more importantly, by your knowledge of how to do it.

MONITOR THE REPAIR

There is a solution to this problem. The solution is proper information. Every time you set up a new procedure or system, you must be able to monitor two things: First, has the system been implemented? Second, what are the results? Your monitoring systems must also give you the ability to insure that the new system or procedure is being maintained and followed by all employees — and that means followed exactly as you set it up, without modification.

While doing a turnaround, a new manager discovered that there was no invoice control. Invoices were not accounted for, thereby allowing them to get lost prior to billing. This was a serious problem because the company could end up shipping the merchandise, and for some reason, never sending the customer a bill. This condition also allowed anyone to have a free license to steal. They could enter an order, ship the merchandise, and then remove the invoice from the system before it got posted to the accounts receivable, and no one would be the wiser.

The new manager set up a control system and asked his managers to install it. Thirty days later, in an out-of-the-way conversation, the manager learned that the system was still not in place. He asked why, and was told that they were waiting for some automatic numbering machines to be fixed. The manager explained the importance of the new system and asked once again that the system be installed immediately. Two weeks later, the manager asked if the system was working all right. He was told that the system had not been installed because one of the key girls was on vacation, and that they would start it as soon as she returned. By this time, the new manager was furious.

Finally, the system was installed. Only one thing went wrong. The girl responsible for keeping track of the numbers did it on a time-available basis and sometimes she did not post them at all. The result was just about the same as not having the system at all. This is typical of what actually happens when there is a lack of support information and accountability.

What was wrong with the way things went in the above scenario? The first thing that was wrong was the lack of a clear-cut assignment of responsibility. With responsibility comes accountability.

How was the problem perceived by the other managers? They needed to understand how important it was to solve. Only two people understood that there was a problem in the first place. Therefore, step number one should have been communication and people involvement. Gather the people involved in working with the system and fixing the problem. Share with them the problem as you understand it. Explain why it is important. Then they should have an opportunity to review the possible solution to see if they feel it can work or add possible improvements.

The next step should have been to outline the tasks involved, assign specific people to be responsible and place a time-frame on the project. It is very important for everyone to agree to the commitment. Moreover, everyone should receive a copy of the plan, so that they can see it in its entirety and refer to it if necessary.

The final step is to have someone prepare a progress report at specified milestones. This information will let the manager know if there were any snags or if someone on the team is holding up the project. It also forces others to understand that they are accountable.

Then, at a predetermined point, audit the new system to insure that it is working as designed. The audit can be very simple, as long as it gives you the confidence that the problem is solved and the system is performing. The audit should be in the form of a written report or memo.

If the audit indicates that there are still problems, then of course, modifications will be necessary, or the process will have to start over again.

When a project or problem is handled in the above fashion, two major things occur. Your involvement becomes that of a leader, as it should be, and you put the responsibility squarely on the shoulders of those people who must carry it out. As a leader, your contribution to management is at its maximum value. You are truly doing work that is worthy of your position and responsibility, and not doing work that can be accomplished by clerical personnel.

It also establishes a system of accountability. With this system, you no longer have to keep track of all the projects and where they are on the completion list in your head. That responsibility falls directly on those people to whom you assign those projects. With your mind free, you can concentrate on other projects and new ideas.

Insist on these progress reports. Otherwise, you will be virtually in the dark, and just like the manager in the scenario, you will discover that what you thought was happening is not happening.

REPORTS ON OPERATIONS

The information needed on projects is quite different from the information you need about operations. While projects require progress reports, operations require specific, interim numbers—numbers that can tell you how things are going. They are the kind of numbers that suggest trends or give you assurance that the business is running on target. These numbers are not necessarily the same as those your accountant gives you in a financial statement. Some are, but most cover a different time sequence. They reflect how the operation is doing at a specific point in time. Because of this, they must be very current and must come to you often.

The reason financial statements from your accountant cannot give you this kind of information is because accounting financial statements are usually prepared after the close of a bookkeeping cycle (usually monthly). So, in the best scenario, it will take another 10 to 20 days before you see this information. By that time, it is a post mortem. The information is history, and there is nothing you can do to make corrections in the trend.

In a turnaround, you must respond quickly to adverse situations. You cannot afford to wait 45 to 60 days to find out what happened financially, especially with the cash position, which is not a part of the monthly statements anyway. The information you need to effectively manage or maintain your turnaround goes beyond the information that you would get from your normal accounting source. You need weekly " flash reports."

Chapter 10 discussed the importance of a daily cash flow report. Poor handling of cash flow can destroy all that you have done and put you back into a critical operational mode. Consequently, one of the most important information reports is a timely (no longer than weekly) cash-flow analysis report similar to the example in Chapter 10. Here is another look at it:

BEGINNING CASH BALANCE________________
ACCOUNTS RECEIVABLE PAYMENTS__________
CASH SALES____________________________
CHECKS ISSUED________________________
ENDING CASH BALANCE___________________

Two other very important pieces of information are timely reports of sales and billings. Sales and billings are separate items because each is important on its own merit. Sales are made at the point of taking an order, whereas billings are made at the point of shipping that order. The orders that have been taken and not yet shipped are called "backlog," or in certain situations, "works in process." Backlog or works in process information is also critical because it can tell you about the future expectations of the business operations.

Sales orders booked will eventually become billable sales; therefore, rapid information about booked sales will let you know on a "now" basis what will happen to your income stream at a point in the future. If you can see the booked sales on a weekly basis, you can do something about it as it is happening. In any event, you can cut back operations to meet declining sales trends or gear up for anticipated sales increases.

Billings or shipments are also very important because that is how you create accounts receivable. This is the item called "sales" on your financial statement. Sometimes this is the true measurement of the business. Think about it. One of the first questions someone might ask about your business is, "What is your sales volume?"

The month itself may or may not be good, depending on what your billings were, because all the fixed expense and overhead are factored into a one-month cycle. Viewing the billings on a weekly basis will give you the rapid information needed to take the pulse of the operation. Based on the information in these reports, you can determine what action to take.

Finally, backlog information can be used as a measurement of operational efficiency. For example, if sales decrease and the backlog increases, what does that tell you? You might want to focus on why the organization is not getting the shipments out. What if sales increase and backlog increases? Perhaps you should consider beefing up the organization to increase the billings proportionate to the sales. Remember, you can not pay your bills with sales and backlog. You must have billings. However, if you do not have sufficient sales and backlog, eventually you will not have enough accounts receivable collections to pay your bills either. It all takes a balance of flow, and, as the manager, you must have a handle on that flow. No financial statement can help you fix something when that information comes too late. The following sample report can give you a weekly indication of that flow. You can then determine how you want it to balance, and because that information is very current you have the unique opportunity to do something about it *now*.

The following is an example of typical information. Your particular business may have additional information that is important, such as bid dollars or estimates rendered.

SALES AND BACKLOG REPORT

REPORT FOR THE MONTH OF__________ WEEK #_____

BEGINNING BACK LOG $____________

SALES THIS WEEK $________ SALES MONTH TO DATE $_________

BILLING THIS WEEK $______ BILLINGS MONTH TO DATE $_____

ENDING BACK LOG $______________

The manager who looks at a piece of information must be able to determine what that information is telling him. Otherwise it is useless information. In the above report, you should be concerned with comparative relationships. For example, are the sales and billings running the same this week? That means the backlog will remain the same. If sales and billings and backlog change with respect to each other, what are the causes? Is there a trend developing (good or bad)?

The key is to keep the reports simple and to have them provide only the type of information that can allow you to acquire an instant picture of what the business is doing in that area of concern. Having piles and piles of computer reports can only bog you down and eat up the limited time you have to zero in on the relevant information. If this is the only way to extract the information, then have a clerical person read through those reports and produce, for you, a simple report similar to the one shown above.

There are three other pieces of information that are also extremely important. They are: accounts receivable, inventory, and payroll status. Accounts receivable and inventory are important, because they represent large dollars of investment; payroll is important, because it is, most likely, your largest expense item.

Here are a few simple reports to give you a rapid picture of what is going on in these areas:

INVENTORY REPORT

***INFORMATION FOR THE MONTH OF*______________**

BEGINNING INVENTORY $ ________LAST MO. SALES $____________

ENDING INVENTORY $____________INCREASE/DECREASE $_______

NUMBER OF TURNS THIS MONTH __________ SALES $ ____________

PAYROLL REPORT

FOR THE MONTH OF ___________

P/R WEEK OF _______$________ OVERTIME HRS._____ $________

P/R MONTH TO DATE $__________ MTD O/T HRS. _____ $________

P/R WEEK OF _______$________ OVERTIME HRS._____ $________

P/R MONTH TO DATE $___________ MTD O/T HRS. _____ $________

P/R WEEK OF _______$________ OVERTIME HRS._____ $_________

P/R MONTH TO DATE $___________MTD O/T HRS. _____ $_________

P/R WEEK OF _______$________ OVERTIME HRS._____ $_________

P/R MONTH TO DATE $__________ MTD O/T HRS. _____ $_________

TOTAL PAYROLL $__________ LAST MONTH PAYROLL $__________

TOTAL OVERTIME HRS. _______ LAST MONTH TOTAL HRS._______

TOTAL OVERTIME $ ___________ LAST MONTH TOTAL $_________

ACCOUNTS RECEIVABLE REPORT

FOR THE MONTH OF ____________

TOTAL A/R $_______DAYS____ LAST MONTH $________DAYS_____

SALES FOR THE WEEK OF _____ COLLECTIONS $________%_______

SALES FOR THE WEEK OF _____ COLLECTIONS $________%_______

SALES FOR THE WEEK OF _____ COLLECTIONS $________%_______

SALES FOR THE WEEK OF _____ COLLECTIONS $________%_______

SALES FOR THE WEEK OF _____ COLLECTIONS $________%_______

TOTAL SALES $__________TOTAL COLLECTIONS $________%_____

REVIEW

To summarize, some of the basics of information gathering are:

1. Get quick, pertinent information on a regular basis.
2. Manage projects differently from operations.
3. Assign responsibility.
4. Monitor accountability.
5. Look at weekly flash reports to monitor the trends.

Some businesses get into trouble in the first place because managers do not get proper information on a timely basis. Most turnarounds fall short of success because managers will not take the time to insure that the proper information is forthcoming and that the information is acted upon in a timely way.

PHASE FOUR: TURNAROUND

Phase four, the final phase, does not always happen. Sometimes, the story ends with phase three. However, if the story continues to phase four, then the following usually takes place: the owner, either by himself or with the help of a consultant or new general manager, prepares a turnaround plan. The plan includes many of the techniques and ideas presented in this book. The plan is then sold to the players involved, such as the employees, suppliers, banks, and customers if necessary.

Phase four can be a lot of fun. The reason it can be fun is because of the excitement generated. This is the motivation that we are talking about. The longer and more complete this motivation is, the better the chances are for success. As a result, you must pay careful attention to the motivational aspect of the turnaround.

If done improperly, some adverse effects can be forthcoming. For example, there is the story of a wholesale company that ran into some financial difficulties. The owner was a brilliant motivator and a very exciting person himself. In the initial stages of the turnaround, he was able to muster the support of everyone involved, especially his employees. They approached the turnaround challenges in a manner that most employees will adopt: they worked harder and took pay cuts. That was just fine, because they felt they were fighting for survival. They were able to view the reality in the light of their own survival. They took a proprietary interest in seeing that the business survived for the business's sake as well as for their own. They never felt they were working for the owner alone. They were working for themselves.

This transfer of interests worked wonders for the turnaround. As a result, the company survived and started to turn around, slowly at first. The employees continued this labor of love for about six months. It became clear that the turnaround was working, and it appeared that the company was going to survive. The owner knew this, but instead of using the good news to keep the excitement going, he kept silent. All he would say is, "We are starting to do all right."

It was true; the company was starting to do well — well enough to pay off some of the loans acquired during the critical financing stage. The owner now had some breathing room and could invest some money in machinery and sales promotion. He then hired some additional people in the sales and marketing departments, supplying them with cars and expenses. He also took a well deserved and needed vacation in the Bahamas. The employees saw all this and became concerned.

The more the business recovered, the more the owner stopped communicating with the employees. He did, however, tell his suppliers and bankers that the situation was in hand and that the company was, in fact, turned around. The owner ran the company just as if nothing had happened; as if there was never a turnaround. As far as he was concerned, it was business as usual.

Try to imagine how this went over with the employees. The longer the owner behaved as if nothing had happened, the worse the employees felt. They talked among themselves, and their anger increased. Some of the more aggressive employees approached the owner about the turnaround. He told them that everything was back to normal. When they asked about their pay cuts and benefit reductions, the owner said he could not do anything about that or the company would get into trouble again. Three weeks later, the owner's auto lease expired, so he got a new car.

By now, the employees were thinking they had been had. The warehouse manager eventually left the company, taking a few other key employees. The employees that stayed lost their enthusiasm for the company and a morale problem developed. The owner did not realize what was happening. He was back in phase one again. The company slid backward and was in a mini-turnaround again. Unfortunately, this time the owner could not go to his employees for help, nor could he generate any enthusiasm for fixing the problems. The company went on just barely breaking even for about two years. Sales were stagnant as well. Then, a recession hit the company, as it did so many others. The company did not survive this time.

KEEP THE ENTHUSIASM GOING

A turnaround cannot be abruptly stopped. It must continue. As the condition improves, employees, creditors, and anyone else involved must be told the good news. Good news begets good news. Everyone likes to win, and everyone likes to be associated with a winner. Build on that. Let every small victory be proclaimed. Eventually, small victories become big victories. When they do, reward the participants. This encourages them to do even more, instead of what happened in the above story where the absence of reward discouraged the employees. The reward does not have to be large; it just has to be proportionate to the victory. For example:

There is the story of a printing company that produced the election ballots for its county each year. For the past few years, the company had lost money every time they did the job. (It was a very large order.) When the company got into trouble, they hired a new chief operating officer. When the ballots came up for bid again, he asked his employees to rebid the job with a profit in mind. Some complained that if the price was too high they would lose the order to competition. The new boss was unwavering. He told them that the company needed the order, but only if it could make a profit. He also told them that, if the company made a profit on the order, the key employees involved would receive a little something extra.

The employees prepared a bid that included some serious savings they felt they could achieve. When they got the job, the new boss outlined a program of incentive rewards based on how much profit they made. The more the profit, the bigger the bonus. Sure enough, the company made the largest profit ever on that particular job. The county was so happy about the performance that they wrote a testimonial letter to the new boss and complimented him on what a great job his employees had done. The rewards were given with pomp and ceremony, and a great deal of motivation was realized.

WHAT MOTIVATES PEOPLE

Psychologists are frequently asked, "How do I motivate my salespeople or employees?" There is an answer to the question, but it is a complicated one. You must first examine the motivating factors for all human beings.

People have certain specific human needs which change depending upon their present circumstances. For example, the very basic and universal human needs are physiological. Most animals, whether human or not, require food, shelter and other needs related to the most basic level of survival, which includes procreation. Each human being is different, and the level of an individual's physiological needs may vary from person to person. Some require more, and some require very little. The common ingredient is that, once a person has achieved those basic needs, he no longer can be motivated by them unless they are threatened. This is why fear can be a motivation device.

FEAR AND PUNISHMENT

Fear is a potent motivator. For example, suppose an employee's job is threatened as a result of his excessive absenteeism. The employee responds favorably to the fear motivator, because he does not want to get fired. He changes his behavior and does not miss any more work, because, if he gets fired, he endangers his ability to provide food and shelter. Here, fear works as a motivational technique.

What if that same employee is not concerned about losing his job, because he is financially independent or has enough money in the bank to remove the sense of immediate concern over the basic element of survival? Obviously, the motivational technique of fear will not work.

The point of the matter is this: What motivates one person will not necessarily motivate another.

The fear motivator need not always be the ultimate punishment, the loss of a job. Fear should be used cautiously, because, when fear is used with frequent application, it builds resentment. An employee will eventually consider the possible threat itself as a reason to protect himself, which could result in unwanted turnover.

Fear can operate subliminally. For example, your written company policy on absenteeism, sick time, tardiness, theft, and all the things you want your employees to do or not do work for you in a positive way. Fear is the motivational device. Break the rules, suffer the consequences.

REWARDS

What about reward? How does that fit in? It sounds like a better way to motivate people, doesn't it? Actually, as a motivation technique, it is no better or worse than fear; it just works differently, and it works for different reasons. Just like fear, rewards also have limited motivational adequacy.

What human needs does reward appeal to? For certain people, it can appeal to one of the basic physiological needs when money is the reward. But what happens to those people who do not need money? You say that everyone needs money. That is true to some extent, but money is no longer used for the basic physiological needs of food and shelter. Money has other motivational value.

There are two other components involved. One is the human need for security, and the other is the human need for recognition. When it comes to security, money can furnish the feeling of independence, which, in turn, makes one feel very secure. With regard to recognition, money can buy the medals of acknowledgment, such as a new car, expensive clothes, jewelry, or a big house. These things, very often, are perceived by the holder to say, "Look at me—I'm successful." Therefore, the giving of money as a reward works well, because each individual can give himself the kind of medal that he needs.

There is one problem with using money as a reward. Once it becomes expected, it no longer has great motivational strength.

Money is sometimes used as the exclusive motivator for salespeople. This strategy is erroneous in its concept, because salespeople will be motivated by money only to the same degree that anyone else is. After awhile, the incentive disappears, and the salespeople consider the rewards as part of their compensation package. The abrogation of commission for a straight salary is not recommended. On the contrary, salespeople need a heavily-weighted commission program, one that encourages production. Nevertheless, salespeople need other rewards above and beyond commissions, and these rewards can motivate them to achieve superior results.

RECOGNITION

The recognition aspect for motivating people is significant, because it can never be entirely satisfied as physiological needs can. This means you can use it to motivate people without fear of overdoing it or wasting the reward. Certificates, plaques, testimonial lunches or dinners are very effective motivational strategies also. For example, an "employee of-the-month" program is one of these motivational stratagems. A good system of recognition rewards can be very effective in team building and a great help in maintaining an elevated morale.

To illustrate this principle, there is a story of how a new CEO used rewards and recognition to build enthusiasm at an office supply company that was in financial difficulty. He quickly recognized that the difficulties of the company had taken their toll on the employees, who, as a result, had lost their enthusiasm and spirit. Out of frustration, they gave up trying to get things fixed. To remedy the condition, the new CEO installed a program whereby employees were encouraged to make suggestions for improving the operation or saving the company money. Twenty-five dollars was paid for each suggestion used. Along with the cash award, the winners received a special appreciation certificate. (To some, the certificate was more valuable than the money.)

More than 50 suggestions were turned in during the first 30 days. The quality of most of those suggestions was sound. The second 30 days proved almost as successful, and another 10 suggestions were used. As soon as the program yielded the desired outcome, it was discontinued before it became just another one of those ongoing, low-priority company programs. It was also discarded to make room for other motivational programs.

THE NEED FOR ACCEPTANCE

Acceptance is another one of those human needs that can never be entirely satisfied. This powerful need is why peer pressure is so effective and why it can have a catastrophic consequence on your business when it works against you.

For example, if your organization's culture makes it socially unacceptable for an individual to be conscientious, then some of your best people will hold back because of the fear of being ostracized by their peers.

The goal is to set up an environment that is supportive to the cause of the turnaround. With this as your objective, you can establish a peer culture that forces everyone, committed or not, to respond to the organizational needs of the business.

The best way to get this attitude across is to search out the employee leaders and enlist them to your cause. These leaders may not be your management team. They may be ordinary employees who have the respect and loyalty of their peers.

A "Quality Circle Group" is one of the techniques used for this purpose. Another is called an "Employee Advisory Committee." What you call your group is immaterial as long as it gets these people together to share the problems, the aspirations, the successes, and the failures. It may not even be necessary for them to contribute anything. Their real value comes back to the organization in the way they behave in their environment. Eventually, the underground culture of your organization will respond favorably, and a new, goal-oriented enthusiasm will be pervasive.

THE ULTIMATE MOTIVATION

The ultimate motivation requires no technique, because it appeals to the human need to self actualize or to accomplish something. Not many reach this state, however, even low-level employees will be motivated to some extent by this method. This form of motivation requires an attitude change or focus by the employee. Once that takes place, no additional motivation is necessary.

There is a humorous story about the world's greatest motivator who traveled all over the world motivating people. He could motivate anyone. He was the best.

Every Friday afternoon, he would return home from his trips to find his seven-year-old son waiting for him on the steps of their front porch. When the child saw his father, he got excited and yelled, "Daddy, daddy, daddy, I'm so glad to see you!" This routine went on for two years, until one day, when he came home from one of his motivational trips, he found that his son was not waiting for him as usual. He found his son in his bedroom crying his heart out.

He tried to find out why his son was crying and said, "Son, tell me what's wrong."

The boy looked at his father tearfully and said, "Daddy, my pet turtle died!" That little turtle was the most important thing in his son's world.

The father thought a moment and said to himself, "I'm the world's greatest motivator. Surely I can think of something." He thought again, "Let's see, what kind of motivation can I use? Well, there's fear. I can rough him up a little and...no that's no good; he's only a nine-year-old kid. What else?" He thought, " I've got it! I'll use reward. I'll go out today and buy the kid a hundred turtles. Naa," he thought, "what are we going to do with a hundred turtles? There must be something else." And then it came to him. "I know!" he said, "I'll change his attitude!"

"Son," he said, "that wonderful turtle should have a great and glorious funeral. What do you think?" The son looked at his father, and the tears quit flowing.

" Now here is what I want you to do," the father said. "Go upstairs to your mother's closet and get a shoe box. Next, go into your grandmother's room and get some satin from one of her little pillows. Go down into the basement and spray that shoe box gold. After that, I want you to place the satin in the box and put the turtle on top of that satin."

The boy ran upstairs to his mother's room. He found a shoe box containing her $100.00 pair of shoes and threw the shoes on the floor. He ran into his grandmother's room and took her best satin pillow. He ran downstairs, sprayed the box gold and placed the satin pillow neatly in it. When everything was ready, his aunt played "Amazing Grace" on the organ as he placed the little turtle on the satin and started to march.

Just then the turtle moved! The boy looked at his father, then at the turtle, then at his father again. Sure enough, the turtle moved again. He looked back at his father and said, "Dad! Kill it quick!"

Changing attitudes is a motivational technique that can be used very effectively, especially among your higher-level employees. All it requires is you taking the time to honestly communicate with your key people. Give them responsibility, and when they win, even just a little, build upon it and make that winning work for you. Remember, success breeds success.

REVIEW

There are seven important motivational components to consider. They are:

1. Create excitement.
2. Do not leave people in the cold when the business starts to recover.
3. Communicate the good news — any good news — and communicate it often.
4. Use rewards.
5. Give recognition.
6. Let peer pressure work for you.
7. Develop a winning attitude.

When the success appears so distant, it is easy to become discouraged. The solution is to build upon small victories: that big sale, the better purchase contract, getting open account terms from a vendor that had you on COD, saving an employee from quitting. These are little victories, and it takes a series of little victories before the total winning takes place.

Chapter 16

SETTING GOALS

Success does not normally happen by accident. In the broad spectrum, most enterprises or people plan their success to some degree. Even those who do not appear to be planning actually have some grand design, though it may be unconscious.

For example, when an individual starts his career, he usually chooses some direction by the type of education acquired. What a person chooses to study may have some basis in personal aspirations. Achievement of these aspirations has to do with a myriad of success or failure movements. With some, the resolve to succeed is so embedded into their subconscious that, irrespective of the obstacles, they constantly move toward their desired goal.

Most people fail because they have not etched their goals decidedly and firmly into their brain. As a result, their behavior is random and not destined. They must then depend on a serendipitous event to move them in the direction necessary for their success. When that event does not occur, or when they are unable to even recognize the event, they will, very often, fall short of their unconscious goal.

A business is not much different from a person in the way it approaches success. When a business begins, the owner or founders choose to go into a particular business for a reason. Obviously, it is not to fail, so there is a goal, even though it may not be quantified.

That unwritten goal is resident in the subconscious minds of the management. Naturally, it is much more complicated than that, because many things interfere with those original goals. When a business gets into trouble, the overriding goal becomes "survival." At that point, the original intent of the business is obscured and very often forsaken.

A good way to learn about business success is to parrot the successful accomplishments of others and avoid the obvious pitfalls. Use the experiences of others as a guide. "What do the successful companies do?" To begin, one of the activities that successful companies do is "planning." They plan their sales; they plan their finances; and they plan their activities. They gather all the players to help formulate the plan, and, when they are done, they ask for commitment to that plan.

PLANNING

Planning is important at all stages of a turnaround, and the planning changes as the turnaround matures.

In the beginning, the goals and plans are made on a daily or weekly basis. Later, the plans become more defined and long-range. Once planning gets started, it is absolutely necessary to prepare a complete strategy or grand scheme. This scheme should also be a road map, giving management mileposts by which to measure their performance.

In a previous chapter, the method and the significance of soliciting input from your people were discussed. To reiterate, you must make the plan a living part of the total company. In order to do this effectively, you must involve your people totally. Anything less will weaken your program and your ability to reach your goals.

A good plan should focus on the main objectives and how you can accomplish them. Concomitantly, a good plan should be arranged in an orderly fashion and should provide all the employees with a role to act out, a script, so to speak. Finally, a good plan should allow for accountability and measurement.

The following is a list of the business categories that a good plan should address:

1. Sales and profits
2. Personnel
3. Manufacturing or operations
4. Long-range goals

Within each category there should also be a breakdown of the independent elements that make up the broad category. The following example creates a concise plan and shows you how the plan was developed.

CASE HISTORY

The Special Instruments Co. makes and sells (mainly to hospitals) blood pressure measuring devices. It has been in business about three years and, in the last six months, sales have taken a tumble. As a result, profits have disappeared and the losses have been staggering. Cash flow has become critical, and the company is not able to pay its bills on a timely basis.

The company has developed some electronic-type products it can sell for home use. Unfortunately, the units do not work all the time, and the information is not always accurate. Almost all the units that have been sold have come back under the warranty.

The company had four direct salespeople based in strategic locations around the country. They called primarily on hospitals. Because of declining sales, there are only two salespeople left. Recently, competition has become very tough, and management believes that the market is not growing. Some have even suggested that sales of these products have reached a saturation point.

Inventories are too high, because sales are not keeping up with manufacturing. Because of a cash crunch, all advertising and promotions have been discontinued. This action concerns the management, since sales are already suffering.

Many of the instruments were originally sold via a telemarketing program. This was changed when the person in charge was moved into outside sales.

Upon reviewing all the facts, the Board of Directors had an accounting firm plot the financial destiny of the company. It was determined that the company could only last four more months at its current level of operation.

The management and the Board of Directors, together, decided upon a strategy to save the company and put it back on a healthy foundation. Here is the outline of their program:

TURNAROUND OUTLINE

I. Scope

II. Organization

A. Personnel

B. Finance

TURNAROUND OUTLINE cont'd

III. Sales
- **A. Philosophy**
- **B. Forecast**
- **C. Activities**
  - **1. Products**
  - **2. Customers**
  - **3. Distribution**
  - **4. Advertising**
  - **5. Promotions**
  - **6. Long range concerns**

IV. Profit Plan
- **A. Five-year forecast**
- **B. Cash flow projection**

V. Manufacturing
- **A. Strategy**
- **B. Activities**
  - **1. Facilities**
  - **2. Equipment**

VI. Long-range planning

Now the goals and plans must be defined (in writing) by the board and the management team. The following is the finished document constructed from the problems stated earlier in the chapter and the points outlined above.

TURNAROUND BUSINESS PLAN

I. SCOPE

After three years of operation, the company has been able to establish a sound foundation for the existence of the business. It

(more)

has also been a learning exercise. The company is now at the crossroads of its destiny. Continuing its current path will be detrimental to the enterprise; therefore, a new direction must be sought and implemented.

The plan set forth encompasses all phases basic to achieving this new direction. It also sets important goals for the company as a part of its journey on the path to its new horizon.

II. ORGANIZATION

The company is structured with a traditional organizational matrix. However, new direction demands the modification of the organizational structure and a shifting of the personnel involved.

The following is the new Organization Chart:

(The new organization chart would go here)

A. PERSONNEL

There are three major changes in the personnel status. The first is the replacement of the sales manager with a vice president of marketing. The second is the addition of a company controller. The third is replacing the current vice president of manufacturing and his replacement with the current vice president of technical support. Technical support is to be handled by the CEO.

Other personnel changes include the addition of an electronics expert and a technical marketing research person, and a change in status for the two existing salespeople.

The new vice president of marketing will have experience in the medical instruments field and the consumer products field. The position will be recruited by placing ads in the *Wall Street Journal*. The target salary range is $50,000 to $75,000, depending upon the requirements of the candidates.

An assistant with experience in technical market research will be brought on board to assist the new vice president of marketing.

The new company controller will be either a CPA or CMA, with experience in manufacturing cost systems. He will be recruited by contacting a specialized accounting employment agency. The salary range will be between $35,000 to $50,000. The new controller will take charge of the office, accounting department, and administration. He will report directly to the President.

The current position of vice president of technical support will be abandoned, and the person holding that position will replace the current vice president of manufacturing. His duties will be to focus on quality control, scheduling, and plant personnel.

To help the vice president of manufacturing solve some of the electronic problems, a new electronics expert will be added to the staff.

The two existing sales people will be moved into customer service and technical field support.

All these positions will be recruited by using local newspaper ads. The pay scale will vary, depending on the needs and experience of the applicants.

B. FINANCE

The main activity of the accounting department is to standardize the computer system. At present, there are four microcomputers in use throughout the organization, each doing its own thing and not connected or standardized. These include:

1. TRS 80, in the accounting department, doing general ledger, accounts payable, and receivables. The job is not being done adequately nor is it integrated.

2. TRS 80, in the sales department, doing word processing. This use is inadequate, because there seems to be a bottleneck and work is not getting out on a timely basis.

3. Compaq portable, in the warehouse, doing mainly inventory control. The system does not tie into anything, nor does it work accurately due to program problems.

4. Columbia desk model, in the office, used by the main secretary for word processing.

Move the TRS 80 from the accounting department to the sales

department, giving them two micros of the same kind. They can use the same programs and files to eliminate the processing bottleneck.

Move the Compaq portable into the accounting department. Buy a 20 megabyte hard disk model, along with two terminals, and set up a network program allowing for a three-station, multi-user system. Buy new, standard software specifically designed for the industry. Place one terminal in the plant for cost and inventory input. The other two terminals will remain in the accounting department for input of the other integrated accounting functions.

Leave the Columbia desk model with the main secretary. Standardize the word processing programs between the modified Compaq and the Columbia for simplified access to data base files and spreadsheet reports.

III. SALES

Sales in the past six months have dropped substantially. The reasons are many and varied; however, the difficulties have been identified, and they can be corrected. The main focus will come in two efforts: First, rebuild the distribution system of the company. Second, redesign the products to fit the markets targeted.

A. PHILOSOPHY

At present, sales are managed by a direct sales system with full-time sales employees. The major problem with this method is that it requires a much larger salesforce than the company can afford. As a result, the existing, small sales team cannot develop enough volume to reach the necessary sales projections. In order to solve the problem, it is essential that a new sales organization be put in place without expending any financial resources. This will require changing the present sales system from direct sales to sales by manufacturer's representatives.

No matter how great or large the sales organization, there can never be a sales success if the products do not work or if they do not fit the marketplace. Logically, an effort must be made to correct these problems, thereby eliminating the obstacles. This is fundamental in our company philosophy.

B. FORECAST

The sales forecast shows year one through year five and uses last year's results to establish a base. By this method, you can see more clearly what impact a more aggressive sales effort can achieve. A sample sales forecast follows:

SALES FORECAST

YEAR 1	YEAR 2	YEAR 3	YEAR 4	YEAR 5
$813,000.	**$975,600.**	**$1,190,232.**	**$1,594,510.**	**$2,232,875.**

C. ACTIVITIES

In order to reach the forecast, several new activities will take place. These activities cover the entire spectrum of sales and sales development and have been carefully thought out with a view toward attaining results at a minimal expense.

1. PRODUCTS: Non-digital, non-electronic pressure meters now account for approximately 50% of the current company sales. It is a well known industry fact that the future will require more electronic/digital or computerized, blood pressure meters at all distribution levels. At the present time, the company has a good head start on the market by selling a state-of-the-art product.

In order to maximize this market potential, the company must improve the quality control over its present Model 500 (for hospital use). In addition to that, the Model 500 must be modified so that it can be sold less expensively to the physician market as well (Model 300 and an even less expensive Model 200).

We must create two additional versions of the 500, one for the home use and the other for the operating room. The home use model (Model 100) will be inexpensive and easy to operate. The operating-room Model 600 will be totally automated, and Model number 700 will have a computer interface.

The improved, quality version of the original Model 500 will be renumbered as Model 400, and the new Model 500 will also provide hard-copy documentation (similar to the Model 600).

With this wide range of products, virtually all existing markets can be penetrated, increasing future demand for the company's products.

2. CUSTOMERS: The company maintains an active customer list of approximately 5000 names (mainly hospitals). It is estimated that there are more than 65,000 hospitals in the USA, not to mention another 18,000 in Europe and 100,000 small clinics and HMOs across the nation. In addition to the existing markets, new customers will be attracted because of the home use of the product. We estimate there is an attainable, potential market of roughly five million units (Model 100).

The most identifiable potential customer is the physician. It has been determined that each physician's office owns an average of two meters, and there are 250,000 physicians in the USA. This market could render sales of at least 300,000 units within two years.

3. DISTRIBUTION: Because there are three distinct, identifiable markets for the company's new product lines, it will be necessary to establish three separate distribution methods. Each method will be handled by a system of independent manufacturer's representatives. The recruiting firm of Dewey and Dewey has been contacted, and they are in the process of selecting manufacturer's representatives in two areas of concentration: the physician and hospital market specialists, and the home market consumer specialists.

Our target is to employ, on a straight commission basis, 15 representatives to cover the country in the traditional medical field. On the other hand, it will only take six major representative firms to cover the nation, calling on the pharmacy and specialty store market.

To augment this new effort, the two existing salespeople will become field technical support representatives working in the field with these manufacturer's representatives, supplying the training and technical support.

The above program will be the major thrust of the company's marketing efforts. However, for the mechanical (non-electronic) pressure meters, we have devised a different scheme.

Because these products have a limited life cycle, it is not in the company's best interests to diminish any of the efforts of our representative organizations by giving them an obsolete product. Yet, those products presently account for about 50% of all sales. In order to continue with these sales, a telemarketing program will be installed to contact present customers to solicit orders for the non-electronic pressure meter.

4. ADVERTISING: Traditionally, aggressive advertising in this field has not proven worthwhile. Yet, some institutional identification is necessary to support the sales efforts in the field. Therefore, most of our programs this year will be in the form of direct mail contact to customers and prospects.

To begin, the existing customers will be set up on a computer data base. From that list, selected mailings will take place bimonthly. A similar program will be set up to contact prospective customers.

5. PROMOTIONS: Most of the promotions will be tied into the direct mail campaigns, with two major campaigns scheduled. The first will be in the form of an announcement for the new, digital electronic line of pressure meters. The second will follow in three months, announcing an inventory reduction sale of the nondigital traditional meters.

We have set aside a small promotional budget for discretionary sales representative use. Funds will also be available to bring potential, large buyers to the factory for indoctrination.

6. LONG-RANGE CONCERNS: For the time being, the method of using manufacturer's representatives suits the company's purpose. It will enable the company to receive the initial sales effort, so vitally needed. Moreover, this sales effort can be accomplished at a fraction of the usual inaugural costs.

The concern is that a typical manufacturer's representative organization handles many other product lines. Will their dedication be abridged because of the pressures that other companies place upon them? If this dilemma materializes, the company must consider the possibility of using a direct salesforce again.

IV. PROFIT PLAN

A. FIVE-YEAR FORECAST

The profit plan has been very carefully thought out and allows for many contingencies. Because of the way the profit plan is designed, it will become the first year's operating budget.

Focusing on year two (this year), we can see that the loss trend has been reversed and that a profit of $51,927.50 will be realized. To achieve this profit goal, we will have to increase sales approximately 20%. Even though this may appear to be aggressive, it is genuinely possible considering all the marketing activities planned.

B. CASH FLOW PROJECTION

The cash flow forecast clearly illustrates a shortage of cash at the sales and operating levels indicated by the profit plan. Therefore, it will be necessary to borrow $50,000 by the middle of the year and another $30,000 at the beginning of following year. By the end of year three, the cash flow will have turned the corner and, once again, become positive. By year five, all loans can be repaid and there will be a cash flow surplus of $427,115.98.

V. MANUFACTURING

A. STRATEGY

It is unfortunate that so little attention has been paid to manufacturing and its facilities. As a result, quality control has disappeared, scheduling does not exist, machinery has gone without maintenance, and the facilities have deteriorated. In order to support the plan and its aggressive sales buildup, it will be necessary to completely redefine and reorganize the entire manufacturing operation.

B. ACTIVITIES

The company is going to add six new products to the line within 15 months. This will require the manufacturing organization to gear up fast to accommodate these activities.

1. The facilities occupy three buildings and provide no possibility for a production line flow. The lease on two of the buildings comes due in the early part of the year. The plan is not to renew but to negotiate out of the lease on the third building. By mid-year, a new facility of about 25,000 square feet should be found. At that time, all the facilities will move onto the new premises.

2. Once the move has been decided upon, a professional designer will be hired to design the placement, to purchase new equipment (as needed), and to supervise construction of the new facilities.

VI. LONG-RANGE PLANNING

The immediate quest is to reposition the company to make and sell state-of-the-art products and to establish a strong distribution team. The long-range target, although it may be realized after the five-year plan, is to enter the "blood" market in a broader way by providing measuring and testing devices. Phase one will begin at the end of year three. In this phase, a serious market research program will explore the many possibilities and zero in on the most favorable opportunities. Feasibility studies on potential new products will occupy most of the R & D during year four. In early year five, at least one new product will be introduced and two more will follow by the end of the year.

By the end of year five, the profits and cash flow will be very substantial. Therefore, in year six, a concentrated effort will be made to acquire another company in a related field that can use the same distribution, or in a field where our products can fit into their distribution. The key factors for an acquisition target will be products, manufacturing, facilities, and distribution network. Any one or a combination of these components will qualify as a target. The goal is to build a company that could become a public offering.

WORK THE PLAN

The preceding business plan is a typical (not elaborate) document designed for one function—the illustration and clarification of goals, and the activities required to reach those goals. Leading a turnaround without this kind of document is like walking on one leg. Yes, it can be done if you are skillful; but think how much easier it would be using both legs.

To illustrate the importance of a written plan, there was this small manufacturing company that went through three phases. In the beginning, it did not have a plan; later, it worked on a defined plan, and then, still later, it abandoned the plan. Here is what happened:

In the early days, the president operated his small business just like thousands of other small business managers, and it was fine. When sales reached the million-dollar level, the owners put a great deal of pressure on the manager (who was also one of the owners) to hire a controller and put the company on a budget. The manager resisted this idea, saying he needed a marketing manager more than an accountant. He won out, and the company hired a marketing manager from the competition.

The competition was a much larger company, and, as a result, had trained its managers to be planners. The new marketing manager came to the company with a good understanding of planning and budgeting. At first, the new marketing manager only addressed the marketing plan. A year later, he produced a marketing budget. A few years later, he became an officer of the corporation, and the entire company had a very defined budget and operating plan. The company grew more than 500% in a period of less than 11 years.

Soon after preparing his last annual plan, the marketing manager (now a vice president) left the company. He felt he had left the company with a full tank of gas (so to speak) and that if those who were left to do his job followed the plan, they should do all right. That year was the best and biggest year in the history of the company.

The company did not hire a replacement. Management believed they could handle the operation with the existing personnel. Because of that, a few things occurred. No marketing or operating plan was ever prepared again. They prepared a budget in an obscure manner, limiting its ability to be used as a tool to measure the success of the activities. (They converted to a flexibile budget.) Management fooled the owners to some extent, because they no longer had a real way to measure the performance of the CEO.

The next year, the company did 10% fewer sales than the previous year, which was something that had never happened before. Six months later, a major problem surfaced. The customers began to rebel. They complained that the company had become undirected, and that no new sales or marketing programs had been implemented in two years. As a consequence of this unusual customer insurrection, sales fell off considerably. It was evident that this would be another year where sales would be 10% less than the year before and 20% down from the time they did away with planning. Profits also fell.

It was finally concluded that the company needed a strong, new direction to turn around the sales and marketing problem.

When you analyze the disorder, you find that the answer lies in a lack of leadership and direction. There is a valuable lesson to be learned from this little story: Never let up, no matter how well things appear to be going. This axiom is even more appropriate in a turnaround.

In the final analysis, the real key to maintaining a turnaround, or any business for that matter, is to plan, plan, and when you are finished planning, plan again. Then work your plan. Be aggressive and fight hard to succeed. Having and working your plan is the best way to be prepared to deal with the turnaround. Remember, even Noah did not wait for the rain before he built the Ark.